Betty Crocker's

Fast and Flavorful

100 Main Dishes You Can Make in 20 Minutes or Less

MACMILLAN • USA

MACMILLAN
A Simon & Schuster Macmillan Company
1633 Broadway
New York, NY 10019

MACMILLAN is a registered trademark of Macmillan, Inc.
BETTY CROCKER and BISQUICK are registered trademarks of General Mills, Inc.

Library of Congress Cataloging-in-Publication data

Crocker, Betty
    Betty Crocker's Fast and Flavorful 100 main dishes you can make in
20 minutes or less — 1st ed.
        p.   cm.
    ISBN 0-02-861985-4
    1. Entrées (Cookery)   2. Quick and easy cookery.   I. Title.
II. Title: Fast and Flavorful 100 main dishes you can make in 20
minutes or less.   III. Title: 100 main dishes you can make in 20
minutes or less.   IV. Title: One hundred main dishes you can make in
20 minutes or less.
TX740.C685   1997
641.8′2—DC21   97-17150
                                                            CIP

GENERAL MILLS, INC.
Betty Crocker Food and Publications Center
Director: Marcia Copeland
Editor: Lori Fox
Recipe Development: Nancy Cooper, Anne Stuart
Food Stylists: Kate Courtney Condon, Katie McElroy, Cindy Lund
Nutritionists: Elyse A. Cohen, M.S., Nancy Holmes, R.D.
Photographer: Steve Olson
Cover design by Iris Jeromnimon
Book design by George J. McKeon

Manufactured in the United States of America
10 9 8 7 6 5 4 3 2 1
First Edition
Cover: Fettuccine with Ricotta, Tomato and Basil (page 90)
Back Cover: Shrimp and Feta Pizza (page 100)

Introduction

Beat the boring dinner blues with *Betty Crocker's Fast and Flavorful*! Turn to Betty Crocker for simple solutions—America's favorite cook is at your side. With *Betty Crocker's Fast and Flavorful,* you'll find all the answers to meet your quick cooking needs. Each of the 100 recipes here can be prepared in 20 minutes or less—start to finish. The recipes are limited to three concise, easy-to-follow instructions, so you won't find any elaborate or complicated techniques to follow. Check out the "Have a Minute?" and "Come and Eat!" tips with each recipe for ideas on how to make meal planning easy and fun.

Of course, the most rewarding part about cooking with *Betty Crocker's Fast and Flavorful* is the delicious taste! Even though these recipes cheat on time, they make up for it with big flavor. Who says short recipes mean bland meals? Not Betty Crocker. You'll find mouthwatering chicken, fish, beef and pork dishes—plus sensational soups, salads, pasta, pizza and more. Choose from homestyle favorites such as Chicken Stew Over Biscuits or Meatballs and Mashed Potatoes. Why not try something fun and new such as Thai Turkey Burrito Sandwiches, Polenta with Italian Vegetables or Pork Cutlets with Apple, Walnut and Gorgonzola Salsa? You'll love every bite of Linguine with Tuscan Vegetable Alfredo Sauce or Chicken Enchilada Pizzas.

Since each recipe has been approved by the Betty Crocker Kitchens, you can count on each dish tasting absolutely delicious.

Betty Crocker

Contents

Fix It Fast!

How can you get out of the kitchen faster? There are many easy ways to speed up preparation of ingredients and cooking. We've suggested many ideas below, and you probably have some quick-cooking tricks up your sleeve as well. With a little planning and organizing, getting out of the kitchen faster will be simple.

KITCHEN TOOLS— THE RIGHT STUFF

It's so true: The right tool for the right job does make your life easier. Timesaving kitchen tools are so helpful to have on hand; consider some of our favorites:

- apple wedger
- self-cleaning garlic press
- spring-loaded ice-cream/cookie scoops
- egg slicer
- fat separator
- nonstick cookware
- vegetable peeler
- kitchen shears (regular and spring-loaded)
- wire whisks
- blender/food processor (large and mini)
- hand mixer
- microwave oven

SPEEDY KITCHEN SECRETS

Do you feel the need for speed? By learning a few techniques to cut corners, you will be a pro when it comes to cooking more quickly! Falling into the "why didn't I think of that?" category, these ideas couldn't be easier.

- Toss frozen or fresh vegetables into the pasta cooking water during the last few minutes of cooking. This is great for one-pan cleanup when making tossed pasta mixtures.
- It's the size that counts. For faster cooking, cut vegetables, meat and poultry into smaller or thinner pieces.
- Need boiling water in a hurry? Start with hot water and cover the saucepan with a lid; it will come to a boil faster.
- Speedier meat loaf can be made by pressing the uncooked meat loaf mixture into muffin tins instead of a loaf pan—you've just cut the baking time in half!

DO IT NOW, SAVE TIME LATER

As long as the cutting board or food processor is out, why not chop up another onion or two and pop them in a freezer bag for another time? Practically speaking, just taking that extra bit of time to prepare really saves you time in the future. And on one of those nights when you'd rather not cook and you're reaching into the freezer, you can thank yourself for thinking ahead! Check out these ideas:

- Chop onions, bell peppers, celery and carrots. Place desired amount in resealable plastic freezer bags or containers with lids, label and date. Freeze up to one month. To use, add directly to food being cooked without thawing.

- Form extra uncooked hamburger patties. Place waxed paper between each patty, wrap tightly, label and date. Freeze up to four months. To use patties, thaw before cooking.

- Cook ground beef and drain. Place desired amount in resealable plastic freezer bags or containers with lids, label and date. Freeze up to three months.

- Make extra meatballs, uncooked or cooked. Arrange meatballs in single layer on baking pan or cookie sheet; freeze. Remove meatballs from baking pan. Place desired amount in resealable plastic freezer bags or containers with lids, label and date. Freeze up to six months. Add cooked meatballs directly from freezer to food being cooked. If using uncooked meatballs, make certain to cook until meatballs are no longer pink in center and juice is clear.

1

QUICK CHICKEN AND FISH

*Southwest Chicken
Skillet (page 12)*

Grilled Caribbean Jerk Chicken with Banana-Peach Chutney

4 SERVINGS

Caribbean jerk seasoning includes red pepper, thyme and allspice all in one little jar! The banana and peach stirred into prepared chutney add a fresh fruit flavor. This chicken can be broiled too. Broil with top of chicken four to six inches away from heat for the same amount of time as in step 2.

Have a Minute?

Spread hot cooked rice on a serving platter and top with chicken and chutney. Garnish with grated lime peel and chopped peanuts.

COME AND EAT!

Add hot cooked rice to serve as a moderator for the spicy chicken.

2 tablespoons Caribbean jerk seasoning

1 tablespoon vegetable oil

2 tablespoons lime juice

4 skinless, boneless chicken breast halves (about 1 pound)

1/2 cup chutney

1 large banana, coarsely chopped

1 large peach, chopped

1. Heat coals or gas grill. Mix jerk seasoning, oil and 1 tablespoon of the lime juice. Rub mixture on chicken.

2. Cover and grill chicken 4 to 6 inches from medium heat 8 to 10 minutes, turning once, until juice is no longer pink when centers of thickest pieces are cut.

3. While chicken is grilling, mix chutney, banana, peach and remaining 1 tablespoon lime juice. Serve chicken with chutney.

1 Serving: Calories 255 (Calories from Fat 65); Fat 7g (Saturated 2g); Cholesterol 60mg; Sodium 80mg; Carbohydrate 25g (Dietary Fiber 2g); Protein 25g.

Spicy Mexican Skillet Chicken

4 SERVINGS

Black beans can be hard to find. Sometimes they're shelved with other canned beans; they're often found with Mexican ingredients. If you can't find them in either location, kidney or pinto beans can be used instead.

1 to 2 teaspoons chili powder

1/4 teaspoon salt

1/4 teaspoon pepper

4 skinless, boneless chicken breast halves (about 1 pound)

1 tablespoon vegetable oil

1 can (15 ounces) black beans, rinsed and drained

1 cup frozen whole kernel corn

1/3 cup thick-and-chunky salsa

Chopped fresh cilantro, if desired

1. Mix chili powder, salt and pepper. Sprinkle evenly over both sides of chicken breast halves.

2. Heat oil in 10-inch skillet over medium heat. Cook chicken in oil 8 to 10 minutes, turning once, until juice is no longer pink when centers of thickest pieces are cut.

3. Stir in beans, corn and salsa. Heat to boiling; reduce heat to low. Cover and simmer 3 to 5 minutes or until vegetables are hot. Sprinkle with cilantro.

1 Serving: Calories 305 (Calories from Fat 65); Fat 7g (Saturated 2g); Cholesterol 60mg; Sodium 480mg; Carbohydrate 34g (Dietary Fiber 8g); Protein 34g.

Have a Minute?

Sprinkle with cilantro and serve with lime wedges to squeeze on top.

COME AND EAT!

Hot corn bread with a drizzle of honey is all that's needed to make this meal complete.

Southwest Chicken Skillet

4 SERVINGS

Crush the tortilla chips neatly and easily by placing them in a heavy-duty plastic bag and roll with a rolling pin until coarsely crushed.

Have a Minute?

Stir one small can of sliced ripe olives into the vegetable mixture in step 2.

COME AND EAT!

For a quick salad, top shredded lettuce with a scoop of guacamole and sprinkle with chopped tomato. Flan for dessert? Yes! Top servings of vanilla pudding with warmed caramel ice-cream topping and sprinkle with cinnamon.

1 tablespoon vegetable oil

1 pound skinless, boneless chicken breast halves, cut into 1-inch pieces

1 package (16 ounces) frozen corn, broccoli and red peppers

1 can (15 ounces) black beans, rinsed and drained

1 cup thick-and-chunky salsa

2 cups coarsely crushed tortilla chips

1 cup shredded Cheddar cheese (4 ounces)

1. Heat oil in 10-inch skillet over medium-high heat. Cook chicken in oil, stirring occasionally, until brown.

2. Stir in vegetables, beans and salsa; reduce heat to medium. Cover and cook 6 to 8 minutes, stirring occasionally, until vegetables are crisp-tender.

3. Sprinkle with tortilla chips and cheese. Cover and cook about 2 minutes or until cheese is melted.

1 Serving: Calories 585 (Calories from Fat 225); Fat 25g (Saturated 9g); Cholesterol 90mg; Sodium 960mg; Carbohydrate 58g (Dietary Fiber 13g); Protein 45g.

Chicken Picante

4 SERVINGS

2 tablespoons margarine or butter

1 pound skinless, boneless chicken breast halves, cut into 1-inch pieces

1 medium zucchini, sliced (2 cups)

1 cup sliced mushrooms (3 ounces)

2 1/2 cups picante sauce or salsa

2 teaspoons sugar

1. Melt margarine in 10-inch skillet over medium heat. Cook chicken in margarine 4 minutes, stirring occasionally.

2. Stir in zucchini and mushrooms. Cook, stirring occasionally, until chicken is no longer pink in center and vegetables are tender.

3. Stir in picante sauce and sugar. Cook about 5 minutes, stirring occasionally, until hot.

1 Serving: Calories 230 (Calories from Fat 80); Fat 9g (Saturated 3g); Cholesterol 60mg; Sodium 580mg; Carbohydrate 14g (Dietary Fiber 4g), Protein 27g.

Have a Minute?

Make corn muffins using a package mix. Stir in 1/2 cup shredded sharp Cheddar or Monterey Jack cheese with jalapeño peppers into the batter.

COME AND EAT!

Serve the zesty chicken mixture over split corn muffins. Fresh fruit or cut-up raw vegetables as a side dish would add a refreshing crunch.

Italian Beans with Chicken

4 SERVINGS

1 tablespoon olive or vegetable oil

1 pound skinless, boneless chicken breast halves, cut into 1-inch pieces

1 clove garlic, finely chopped

1/2 cup chopped drained oil-packed sun-dried tomatoes

1/4 cup sliced ripe olives

1 tablespoon chopped fresh or 1 teaspoon dried basil leaves

2 cans (15 to 16 ounces each) cannellini or great northern beans, rinsed and drained

1. Heat oil in 10-inch skillet over medium heat. Cook chicken and garlic in oil about 5 minutes, stirring occasionally, until chicken is no longer pink in center.

2. Stir in remaining ingredients. Cook, stirring frequently, until hot.

1 Serving: Calories 415 (Calories from Fat 90); Fat 10g (Saturated 2g); Cholesterol 60mg; Sodium 610mg; Carbohydrate 50g (Dietary Fiber 12g); Protein 43g.

Have a Minute?

Canned, quartered artichoke hearts (drained) can be added in step 2.

COME AND EAT!

Serve with crusty Italian or French bread and a simple tossed salad. A light, fruit-flavored sorbet would be an excellent dessert.

Chicken-Vegetable Couscous

6 SERVINGS

Couscous is a granular form of pasta, but is often used as a grain such as rice. Couscous cooks in five minutes—perfect for meals when you are pressed for time.

Have a Minute?

Shave fresh Parmesan cheese over the couscous instead of the grated cheese and garnish with fresh, whole oregano leaves.

COME AND EAT!

Serve with a crisp romaine lettuce salad tossed with ripe olives and Italian dressing.

1 tablespoon olive or vegetable oil

1 pound skinless, boneless chicken breast halves, cut into 1-inch pieces

2 large tomatoes, chopped (2 cups)

1 small red bell pepper, chopped (1/2 cup)

8 medium green onions, chopped (1/2 cup)

1 clove garlic, finely chopped

1 tablespoon chopped fresh or 1 teaspoon dried oregano leaves

1 teaspoon paprika

1 can (15 to 16 ounces) garbanzo beans, rinsed and drained

5 cups hot cooked couscous or rice

1/4 cup grated Parmesan cheese

1. Heat oil in 10-inch skillet over medium heat. Cook chicken in oil about 5 minutes, stirring occasionally.

2. Stir in remaining ingredients except couscous and cheese; cook 4 to 5 minutes or until vegetables are crisp-tender.

3. Serve over couscous. Sprinkle with cheese.

1 Serving: Calories 390 (Calories from Fat 70); Fat 8g (Saturated 2g); Cholesterol 45mg; Sodium 610mg; Carbohydrate 57g (Dietary Fiber 7g); Protein 30g.

Vegetable Chicken Stir-Fry

4 SERVINGS

Stir-fry sauces are available in many varieties, from salty to sweet and mild to hot and spicy. Look for them in the Asian section of your supermarket.

2 tablespoons vegetable oil

1 pound skinless, boneless chicken breast halves or thighs, cut into 1-inch pieces

3 cups cut-up assorted vegetables (bell peppers, broccoli flowerets, shredded carrots)

1 clove garlic, finely chopped

1/2 cup stir-fry sauce

1. Heat 1 tablespoon of the oil in 12-inch skillet or wok over high heat. Add chicken; stir-fry about 3 minutes or until no longer pink in center. Remove from skillet.

2. Heat remaining 1 tablespoon oil in skillet. Add vegetables and garlic; stir-fry about 2 minutes or until vegetables are crisp-tender. Add chicken and stir-fry sauce. Cook and stir about 2 minutes or until hot.

1 Serving: Calories 250 (Calories from Fat 110); Fat 12g (Saturated 2g); Cholesterol 60mg; Sodium 690mg; Carbohydrate 12g (Dietary Fiber 2g); Protein 25g.

Have a Minute?

Add toasty crunch with toasted wonton skins! Cut wonton skins into thin strips and bake at 350° for 5 to 7 minutes or until light golden brown. Top each serving with whole or broken toasted wonton strips.

COME AND EAT!

Check out the selection of frozen appetizers such as egg rolls or potstickers at the supermarket—they can turn ordinary dinners into special dinners.

Chicken Stew Over Biscuits

4 SERVINGS

The use of refrigerated Alfredo sauce makes old-fashioned comfort food in just fifteen minutes.

Have a Minute?

Toss in 1 cup of sliced celery in step 1 for its flavor and crunch.

COME AND EAT!

Instead of a lettuce salad, make a simple salad of sliced apples or pears. If you would like, sprinkle with walnuts or pecans and a dash of cinnamon.

1 tablespoon vegetable oil

1/2 teaspoon dried thyme leaves

1/4 teaspoon salt

1/4 teaspoon pepper

1 pound skinless, boneless chicken breast halves, cut into 1-inch pieces

1 package (16 ounces) frozen mixed vegetables

1 container (10 ounces) refrigerated Alfredo sauce

1/2 teaspoon Dijon mustard

8 baking powder biscuits

1. Heat oil, thyme, salt and pepper in 10-inch nonstick skillet over medium-high heat. Cook chicken in oil mixture, stirring occasionally, until no longer pink in center.

2. Stir in remaining ingredients except biscuits; reduce heat to medium. Cover and cook 5 to 6 minutes, stirring occasionally, until hot.

3. Split open biscuits. Serve stew over biscuits.

1 Serving: Calories 835 (Calories from Fat 475); Fat 53g (Saturated 19g); Cholesterol 115mg; Sodium 1290mg; Carbohydrate 59g (Dietary Fiber 7g); Protein 38g.

Easy Curried Chicken and Couscous

4 SERVINGS

Instant white rice can be substituted for the couscous. To do so, follow the same directions in step 1, but increase the water to two cups and substitute two cups uncooked instant rice for the couscous.

Have a Minute?

Curries often have a hint of sweetness, so if you'd like, stir 1/4 cup of raisins into the mixture in step 3.

COME AND EAT!

Slice a purchased angel food cake loaf into slices. Mix your favorite fruit yogurt with an equal amount of nondairy whipped topping and spoon over cake slices. Top with berries or sliced fruit like peaches or nectarines.

1 3/4 cups water

1 cup uncooked couscous

1 can (10 3/4 ounces) condensed cream of chicken soup

1/2 cup water

1 1/2 teaspoons curry powder

2 cups cut-up cooked chicken

1 cup frozen mixed vegetables, thawed

1. Heat 1 3/4 cups water to boiling in 10-inch skillet. Stir in couscous; remove from heat. Cover and let stand about 5 minutes or until water is absorbed.

2. Remove couscous to large serving platter; keep warm.

3. Heat soup, 1/2 cup water, the curry powder, chicken and vegetables to boiling in same skillet; reduce heat to low. Cover and simmer 3 to 5 minutes or until vegetables are tender. Pour chicken mixture over couscous.

1 Serving: Calories 380 (Calories from Fat 90); Fat 10g (Saturated 3g); Cholesterol 60mg; Sodium 620mg; Carbohydrate 49g (Dietary Fiber 5g); Protein 29g.

Sweet-and-Sour Chicken

4 SERVINGS

1 package (10 ounces) frozen breaded fully cooked chicken chunks

1/4 cup water

1 package (16 ounces) frozen broccoli, carrots and water chestnuts

1 can (20 ounces) pineapple chunks, drained

1 jar (9 ounces) sweet-and-sour sauce (1 1/4 cups)

1. Prepare chicken chunks as directed on package.

2. While chicken is baking heat water to boiling in 3-quart saucepan. Add vegetables; reduce heat to medium. Cover and cook 5 to 6 minutes or until hot; drain.

3. Stir chicken, pineapple and sweet-and-sour sauce into vegetables. Cook over medium heat 3 to 4 minutes, stirring occasionally, until hot.

1 Serving: Calories 370 (Calories from Fat 115); Fat 13g (Saturated 4g); Cholesterol 40mg; Sodium 710mg; Carbohydrate 49g (Dietary Fiber 4g); Protein 18g.

Have a Minute?

Sprinkle with toasted sesame seeds just before serving for a crunchy, nutty flavor.

COME AND EAT!

Serve this Asian favorite with hot cooked rice and a crisp green salad.

Mexican Chicken Burgers

4 SERVINGS

1 pound ground chicken or turkey

1 envelope (about 1 1/2 ounces) taco seasoning mix

4 slices (1 ounce each) Monterey Jack cheese

4 hamburger buns, split

1 avocado, sliced

1/4 cup thick-and-chunky salsa

1. Heat coals or gas grill. Mix chicken and seasoning mix. Shape mixture into 4 patties, each about 3/4 inch thick.

2. Cover and grill patties 4 to 6 inches from medium heat 14 to 16 minutes, turning once, until chicken is no longer pink in center.

3. Top each patty with cheese slice. Cover and grill 1 to 2 minutes longer or until cheese begins to melt. Serve on buns topped with avocado and salsa.

1 Serving: Calories 465 (Calories from Fat 205); Fat 23g (Saturated 9g); Cholesterol 95mg; Sodium 960mg; Carbohydrate 33g (Dietary Fiber 5g); Protein 36g.

Have a Minute?

Brush cut sides of hamburger buns with melted margarine or butter and sprinkle with a little of the taco seasoning mix or chili powder. Grill the buns for 2 to 4 minutes or until lightly browned.

COME AND EAT!

Serve with tortilla chips or potato salad. For southwestern flavor, stir corn, canned green chilies and sliced ripe olives into the potato salad.

Red Pepper—Turkey Rolls

4 SERVINGS

If turkey breast slices are not available, you can substitute flattened chicken breasts.

Have a Minute?

Marinate turkey breast slices in the sauté sauce for 1/2 hour before assembling turkey rolls.

COME AND EAT!

Fresh asparagus and cooked linguine or fettuccine complement these colorful turkey rolls.

4 uncooked turkey breast slices, about 1/4 inch thick

1/4 teaspoon salt

1/4 teaspoon pepper

1/2 medium red or green bell pepper, cut into 8 strips

4 green onions, cut into 4-inch lengths

2 tablespoons vegetable oil

1/2 cup country Dijon chicken sauté sauce (from 9.2-ounce bottle)

1. Sprinkle both sides of turkey slices with salt and pepper. Place 2 bell pepper strips and 1 green onion piece on center of each slice. Tightly roll turkey slice around peppers and onion; fasten with toothpick.

2. Heat oil in 10-inch nonstick skillet over medium-high heat. Cook turkey rolls in oil until brown on all sides.

3. Add sauté sauce. Heat to boiling; reduce heat to medium. Cover and cook 2 to 3 minutes, turning at least once, until turkey is no longer pink in center.

1 Serving: Calories 205 (Calories from Fat 90); Fat 10g (Saturated 2g); Cholesterol 65mg; Sodium 210mg; Carbohydrate 2g (Dietary Fiber 0g); Protein 27g.

Snapper with Sautéed Tomato-Pepper Sauce

4 SERVINGS

For a slightly sweeter-tasting salsa, select a red, yellow or orange bell pepper.

Have a Minute?

Fire up the coals or gas grill and grill the fish over medium heat for 8 to 10 minutes or until it flakes easily with a fork.

COME AND EAT!

A steaming bowl of fresh green beans with a pat of butter and a drizzle of lemon juice would be a good addition.

1 pound red snapper, cod or other lean fish fillets

1 large tomato, chopped (1 cup)

1 small green bell pepper, chopped (1/2 cup)

1 small onion, sliced

2 tablespoons finely chopped fresh cilantro or parsley

1/4 teaspoon salt

1/4 cup dry white wine or chicken broth

1. If fish fillets are large, cut into 4 serving pieces. Spray 10-inch nonstick skillet with cooking spray; heat over medium heat.

2. Arrange fish in single layer in skillet. Cook uncovered 4 to 6 minutes, turning once, until fish flakes easily with fork. Remove fish to warm platter; keep warm.

3. Cook remaining ingredients except wine in same skillet over medium heat 3 to 5 minutes, stirring frequently, until bell pepper and onion are crisp-tender. Stir in wine; cook until hot. Spoon tomato mixture over fish.

1 Serving: Calories 100 (Calories from Fat 10); Fat 1g (Saturated 0g); Cholesterol 50mg; Sodium 230mg; Carbohydrate 5g (Dietary Fiber 1g); Protein 19g.

Cod with Tomato-Olive Sauce

4 SERVINGS

When buying frozen fish, look for packages that are well wrapped and free from ice crystals. Frozen fish should be thawed in the refrigerator or in the microwave.

1 pound cod fillets

1 tablespoon olive or vegetable oil

1 large onion, chopped (1 cup)

1 can (14 1/2 ounces) diced tomatoes with roasted garlic, onion and oregano

1 can (2 1/4 ounces) sliced ripe olives, drained

1/4 teaspoon salt

1/4 teaspoon pepper

2 tablespoons lemon juice

Have a Minute?

Serve with chopped fresh parsley for a bit of color.

COME AND EAT!

This is delicious served with chunks of crusty bread to sop up all of the flavorful juices.

1. If fish fillets are large, cut into 4 serving pieces. Heat oil in 10-inch nonstick skillet over medium-high heat. Cook onion in oil 2 to 3 minutes, stirring occasionally, until crisp-tender.

2. Stir in tomatoes, olives, salt and pepper; heat to boiling. Arrange fish fillets in single layer in tomato mixture. Sprinkle with lemon juice; reduce heat to medium-high.

3. Cover and cook 8 to 10 minutes or until fish flakes easily with fork.

1 Serving: Calories 185 (Calories from Fat 55); Fat 6g (Saturated 1g); Cholesterol 60mg; Sodium 640mg; Carbohydrate 12g (Dietary Fiber 2g); Protein 23g.

Catfish with Pesto

4 SERVINGS

Purchased pesto adds lots of pizzazz to this easy fish dish.

Have a Minute?

Thread red pepper strips through slices of jumbo ripe pitted olives for an elegant touch.

COME AND EAT!

Add warm, cheesy garlic bread, steamed broccoli and fresh strawberries for dessert to complete the meal.

4 catfish, orange roughy or snapper fillets (1 1/2 pounds)
1/4 cup pesto
20 strips roasted bell pepper (from 12-ounce jar)

1. Heat oven to 425°. If fish fillets are large, cut into 4 serving pieces. Place fish in greased square baking dish, 8 × 8 × 2 inches.

2. Spread pesto evenly over each piece of fish. Top each piece with 5 bell pepper strips.

3. Cover and bake about 18 minutes or until fish flakes easily with fork.

1 Serving: Calories 250 (Calories from Fat 110); Fat 12g (Saturated 3g); Cholesterol 95mg; Sodium 200mg; Carbohydrate 2g (Dietary Fiber 0g); Protein 34g.

Catfish with Pesto

Teriyaki Swordfish Kabobs

4 SERVINGS

Celebrate a birthday, a great report card or a well-played game—even on a busy weeknight—with this easy dinner.

Have a Minute?

For a spectacular-looking serving platter, brush the rim with water and sprinkle with chopped fresh parsley. The parsley will adhere to the water. Place kabobs on a bed of orzo pasta or rice in the middle of the platter.

COME AND EAT!

Quickly sauté whole pea pods in a little sesame or vegetable oil and sprinkle with sesame seeds. For dessert, put out whole fresh strawberries and small bowls of sour cream and brown sugar. Dip strawberries into the cool, creamy sour cream and then lightly into the brown sugar.

1/2 cup teriyaki marinade or sauce

1/4 cup orange marmalade

1/2 teaspoon ground ginger

1 pound swordfish or other firm fish fillets, cut into 24 one-inch pieces

1 large unpeeled orange, cut into 8 wedges

1 large red or green bell pepper, cut into 24 chunks

1. Set oven control to broil. Mix teriyaki sauce, marmalade and ginger.

2. Thread fish, orange wedges and bell pepper chunks alternately on each of four 15-inch metal skewers, leaving space between each. Place kabobs on rack in broiler pan. Brush with sauce.

3. Broil with tops about 4 inches from heat 10 to 12 minutes, turning once and brushing with sauce, until fish flakes easily with fork. Discard any remaining sauce.

1 Serving: Calories 230 (Calories from Fat 45); Fat 5g (Saturated 2g); Cholesterol 60mg; Sodium 1440mg; Carbohydrate 26g (Dietary Fiber 2g); Protein 22g.

Grilled Salmon with Hazelnut Butter

4 SERVINGS

Slivered almonds can be substituted for the hazelnuts—they taste great with fish!

Hazelnut Butter (below)

1 pound salmon, halibut or red snapper fillets

1/2 teaspoon salt

1/8 teaspoon pepper

1. Heat coals or gas grill. Prepare Hazelnut Butter.

2. If fish fillets are large, cut into 4 serving pieces. Sprinkle both sides of fish with salt and pepper.

3. Cover and grill fish 4 to 6 inches from medium heat 4 minutes. Turn; spread about 1 tablespoon Hazelnut Butter over each fillet. Cover and grill 4 to 8 minutes longer or until fish flakes easily with fork.

HAZELNUT BUTTER

2 tablespoons finely chopped hazelnuts

3 tablespoons margarine or butter, softened

1 tablespoon chopped fresh parsley

1 teaspoon lemon juice

Spread nuts in shallow bowl or pie plate. Microwave on High 30 seconds to 1 1/2 minutes, stirring once or twice until light brown; cool. Mix hazelnuts and remaining ingredients.

1 Serving: Calories 255 (Calories from Fat 155); Fat 17g (Saturated 4g); Cholesterol 75mg; Sodium 460mg; Carbohydrate 1g (Dietary Fiber 0g); Protein 24g.

Have a Minute?

Go ahead and indulge: Double the recipe for the Hazelnut Butter. Use one batch for grilling and the second to serve with the cooked fish.

COME AND EAT!

Serve with sweet green peas and buttered new potatoes sprinkled with parsley.

Savory Tuna

4 SERVINGS

If you're not tuned in to tuna, swordfish or halibut would be worth a try.

Have a Minute?

Fresh basil leaves and lemon peel curls would be a lovely garnish for the fish.

COME AND EAT!

Nestle fish on a bed of linguine and drizzle with pesto and pan juices. Biscotti cookies, a scoop of cool, creamy ice cream and a steaming latte will be the perfect finish.

1 pound yellowfin tuna, swordfish or halibut 3/4 inch thick

1 teaspoon olive or vegetable oil

1 medium green onion, sliced (2 tablespoons)

1/2 cup pesto

2 tablespoons lemon juice

1. If fish fillets are large, cut into 4 serving pieces. Heat oil in 10-inch nonstick skillet over medium heat. Cook onions in oil 2 to 3 minutes, stirring occasionally, until crisp-tender.

2. Stir in pesto and lemon juice. Top with fish. Heat to boiling; reduce heat to low. Cover and cook 5 to 10 minutes or until fish flakes easily with fork.

1 Serving: Calories 360 (Calories from Fat 235); Fat 26g (Saturated 6g); Cholesterol 50mg; Sodium 160mg; Carbohydrate 3g (Dietary Fiber 1g); Protein 29g.

Tuna Patties with Dilled Sour Cream Sauce

4 SERVINGS

If you're not a tuna lover, a six-ounce can of water-packed, boneless, skinless salmon could be used instead.

Sour Cream Dill Sauce (below)

2 cans (6 ounces each) water-packed tuna, drained

1 1/2 cups cornflake crumbs

1/3 cup mayonnaise or salad dressing

1 medium green onion, sliced (2 tablespoons)

1 teaspoon mustard

1 egg

1 tablespoon vegetable oil

1. Prepare Sour Cream Dill Sauce; set aside.

2. Mix tuna, 1 cup of the cornflake crumbs, 1/3 cup mayonnaise, onion, mustard and egg. Shape mixture into four 4-inch patties. Coat patties with remaining 1/2 cup cornflake crumbs, pressing lightly to coat both sides.

3. Heat oil in 10-inch nonstick skillet over medium-high heat. Cook patties in oil 2 to 3 minutes, turning once, until light golden brown. Serve with Sour Cream Dill Sauce.

SOUR CREAM DILL SAUCE

1/2 cup sour cream

1/4 cup mayonnaise or salad dressing

1 teaspoon dried dill weed

Mix all ingredients in small bowl.

1 Serving: Calories 495 (Calories from Fat 335); Fat 37g (Saturated 9g); Cholesterol 115mg; Sodium 650mg; Carbohydrate 15g (Dietary Fiber 0g); Protein 25g.

Have a Minute?

Serve patties on toasted English muffin halves and top with sauce.

COME AND EAT!

Seasoned rice from a mix and steamed broccoli are perfect accompaniments to this family pleasing meal. Brownies are always a favorite way to finish. How about topping them with canned cherry pie filling and hot fudge sauce?

Sweet-and-Spicy Shrimp

4 SERVINGS

To save time during cooking, mix the soy sauce mixture and arrange all other ingredients on a tray in the order they will be used.

˗Have a Minute?˗

Serve the rice tossed with chopped fresh cilantro and shredded coconut for a Thai flavor.

COME AND EAT!

Desserts can be fun! Dip one-half of fortune cookies into melted chocolate and allow the chocolate to harden.

1/4 cup soy sauce

2 teaspoons sugar

2 teaspoons cornstarch

1/2 teaspoon crushed red pepper

1/2 teaspoon sesame or vegetable oil

1 tablespoon vegetable oil

1 small onion, sliced

1 small green bell pepper, sliced

1 medium carrot, thinly sliced (1/2 cup)

3/4 pound uncooked peeled deveined large shrimp, thawed if frozen

Hot cooked rice, if desired

1. Mix soy sauce, sugar, cornstarch, red pepper and sesame oil; set aside.

2. Heat vegetable oil in 10-inch skillet over medium-high heat. Cook onion, bell pepper and carrot in oil 2 to 3 minutes, stirring occasionally, until crisp-tender.

3. Stir in soy sauce mixture and shrimp. Cook 3 to 5 minutes, stirring occasionally, until shrimp are pink and firm and sauce is thickened. Serve over rice.

1 Serving: Calories 135 (Calories from Fat 45); Fat 5g (Saturated 1g); Cholesterol 120mg; Sodium 1170mg; Carbohydrate 9g (Dietary Fiber 1g); Protein 14g.

Savory Shrimp and Scallops

4 SERVINGS

Sea scallops are the larger scallops, measuring up to 1 1/2 inches, while the small bay scallops measure only 1/2 inch.

-Have a Minute?

Peel the shrimp carefully and leave the tails on—they look prettier and can be eaten by hand if picked up by the tail.

COME AND EAT!

Serve over angel hair pasta or spaghetti with a basket of breadsticks. For a special dessert, drizzle slices of cheesecake with chocolate and butterscotch ice-cream topping.

2 tablespoons olive or vegetable oil

1 clove garlic, finely chopped

1 medium green onion, sliced (2 tablespoons)

2 medium carrots, thinly sliced (1 cup)

1 tablespoon chopped fresh parsley or 1 teaspoon dried parsley flakes

1 pound uncooked peeled deveined medium shrimp, thawed if frozen

1 pound sea scallops, cut in half

1/2 cup dry white wine or chicken broth

1 tablespoon lemon juice

1/4 to 1/2 teaspoon crushed red pepper

1. Heat oil in 10-inch skillet over medium heat. Cook garlic, onion, carrot and parsley in oil about 5 minutes, stirring occasionally, until carrot is crisp-tender.

2. Stir in remaining ingredients. Cook 4 to 5 minutes, stirring frequently, until shrimp are pink and firm and scallops are white.

1 Serving: Calories 275 (Calories from Fat 80); Fat 9g (Saturated 2g); Cholesterol 195mg; Sodium 490mg; Carbohydrate 6g (Dietary Fiber 0g); Protein 43g.

Calypso Shrimp with Black Bean Salsa

4 SERVINGS

The salsa can be prepared and refrigerated up to twenty-four hours ahead of serving time. Peeled and sliced mango can be purchased in cans or in jars, which are located in a refrigerated area of the produce department.

1/2 teaspoon grated lime peel

1 tablespoon lime juice

1 tablespoon vegetable oil

1 teaspoon finely chopped gingerroot

1 clove garlic, finely chopped

1 pound uncooked peeled deveined large shrimp, thawed if frozen

Black Bean Salsa (below)

1. Mix all ingredients except shrimp and Black Bean Salsa in medium nonmetal bowl. Stir in shrimp; let stand 15 minutes.

2. Meanwhile, prepare Black Bean Salsa.

3. Cook shrimp in 10-inch skillet over medium-high heat about 5 minutes, turning shrimp once, until shrimp are pink and firm. Serve shrimp with Black Bean Salsa.

BLACK BEAN SALSA

1 can (15 ounces) black beans, rinsed and drained

1 medium mango, peeled and chopped (1 cup)

1 small red bell pepper, chopped (1/2 cup)

2 medium green onions, sliced (1/4 cup)

1 tablespoon chopped fresh cilantro

1/2 teaspoon grated lime peel

1 to 2 tablespoons lime juice

1 tablespoon red wine vinegar

1/4 teaspoon ground red pepper (cayenne)

Mix all ingredients. Set aside.

1 Serving: Calories 260 (Calories from Fat 45); Fat 5g (Saturated 1g); Cholesterol 160mg; Sodium 410mg; Carbohydrate 36g (Dietary Fiber 8g); Protein 26g.

Have a Minute?

Line individual serving plates with leaf lettuce; spoon salsa over lettuce. Arrange shrimp on salsa.

COME AND EAT!

Serve with a hearty, toothsome bread, such as a sevengrain or peasant sourdough, and a fresh fruit salad using ripe, seasonal fruits.

Scallops Mornay

2 SERVINGS

If fresh asparagus is out of season, use a ten-ounce package of frozen cut asparagus (thawed).

COME AND EAT!

When a truly special meal is in order, team this elegant entrée with a Caesar salad and sourdough bread.

1/4 cup water

1 cup 1-inch pieces fresh asparagus

2 tablespoons margarine or butter

1/2 pound bay scallops

1 tablespoon all-purpose flour

1 teaspoon chopped fresh or 1/4 teaspoon dried tarragon leaves

2/3 cup chicken broth

1/2 cup shredded process Swiss cheese (2 ounces)

1 tablespoon dry sherry or chicken broth

2 cups hot cooked fettuccine or spinach fettuccine

1. Heat water to boiling in 1 1/2-quart saucepan. Add asparagus. Heat to boiling; reduce heat to low. Simmer uncovered about 4 minutes, stirring occasionally, until crisp-tender; drain and remove from saucepan.

2. Melt 1 tablespoon of the margarine in same saucepan over medium-high heat. Cook scallops in margarine 3 to 5 minutes, stirring frequently, until white. Remove scallops from saucepan. Drain liquid from saucepan.

3. Melt remaining 1 tablespoon margarine in same saucepan. Stir in flour and tarragon. Cook over medium heat, stirring constantly, until smooth and bubbly; remove from heat. Stir in broth. Heat to boiling, stirring constantly. Boil and stir 1 minute. Stir in cheese until melted. Stir in scallops, asparagus and sherry. Heat, stirring constantly, just until hot. Do not boil. Serve over fettuccine.

1 Serving: Calories 590 (Calories from Fat 215); Fat 24g (Saturated 8g); Cholesterol 115mg; Sodium 860mg; Carbohydrate 52g (Dietary Fiber 3g); Protein 45g.

Quick Paella

4 SERVINGS

Paella is a contraction of the Spanish words para *and* ella, *meaning "for her." Knowing the origin of the name makes the dish taste even better somehow.*

1/4 cup margarine or butter

1 1/3 cups uncooked instant rice

1 medium onion, finely chopped (1/2 cup)

1/3 cup chopped green bell pepper

2 cloves garlic, finely chopped

1 1/2 cups water

2 cans (8 ounces each) tomato sauce

1 can (6 1/2 ounces) minced clams, drained

1 can (5 ounces) chunk chicken

Pinch of saffron or turmeric, if desired

1. Melt margarine in 10-inch skillet over medium heat. Cook rice, onion, bell pepper and garlic in margarine, stirring occasionally, until rice is light brown.

2. Stir in remaining ingredients. Heat to boiling; reduce heat to low. Simmer uncovered about 5 minutes or until rice is tender.

1 Serving: Calories 365 (Calories from Fat 135); Fat 15g (Saturated 4g); Cholesterol 35mg; Sodium 1000mg; Carbohydrate 44g (Dietary Fiber 3g); Protein 17g.

Have a Minute?

Use fresh clams if they are available in your area.

COME AND EAT!

Paella is really a meal in itself. Offer refreshing lemon sherbet and shortbread cookies for dessert.

TAKE-IT-EASY BEEF AND PORK

Pork Cutlets with Apple, Walnut and
Gorgonzola Salsa (page 53)

Savory Beef Tenderloin

4 SERVINGS

Although presliced mushrooms may be very convenient, try slicing fresh shiitake mushrooms for their more assertive flavor.

Have a Minute?

Smoky, crisply cooked bacon crumbles sprinkled over the beef before serving will leave a memorable impression.

COME AND EAT!

Serve with creamy mashed potatoes and buttered carrots with chopped parsley.

3/4 pound beef tenderloin

2 teaspoons chopped fresh or 1/2 teaspoon dried marjoram leaves

2 teaspoons sugar

1 teaspoon coarsely ground pepper

1 tablespoon margarine or butter

1 cup sliced mushrooms (3 ounces)

1 small onion, thinly sliced

3/4 cup beef broth

1/4 cup dry red wine or nonalcoholic wine

1 tablespoon cornstarch

1. Cut beef into four 3/4-inch slices (beef is easier to cut if partially frozen, about 1 1/2 hours). Mix marjoram, sugar and pepper; rub on both sides of beef slices.

2. Melt margarine in 10-inch skillet over medium heat. Cook beef in margarine 3 to 5 minutes, turning once, until brown. Remove beef to platter; keep warm.

3. Cook mushrooms and onion in drippings in same skillet over medium heat about 2 minutes, stirring occasionally, until onion is crisp-tender. Mix broth, wine and cornstarch in a small bowl; stir into mushroom mixture. Cook over medium heat, stirring constantly, until mixture thickens and boils. Boil and stir 1 minute. Pour over beef.

1 Serving: Calories 165 (Calories from Fat 70); Fat 8g (Saturated 3g); Cholesterol 40mg; Sodium 270mg; Carbohydrate 7g (Dietary Fiber 1g); Protein 17g.

Mexican Steak

4 SERVINGS

Sour cream, cool and smooth, is spooned onto simmered steak strips for a pleasant flavor combination.

1 pound beef tenderloin or boneless top loin steak

1 tablespoon vegetable oil

1 medium onion, chopped (1/2 cup)

1 can (15 ounces) chunky Mexican-style tomato sauce

1 teaspoon chili powder

1 teaspoon ground cumin

1/3 cup sour cream

1 tablespoon chopped fresh parsley or cilantro

1. Cut beef into 1 1/2 × 1/2-inch strips (beef is easier to cut if partially frozen, about 1 1/2 hours). Heat oil in 10-inch skillet over medium-high heat. Cook beef and onion in oil, stirring occasionally, until beef is brown.

2. Stir in tomato sauce, chili powder and cumin. Heat to boiling; reduce heat to low. Cover and simmer about 15 minutes or until beef is tender. Top with sour cream. Sprinkle with parsley.

1 Serving: Calories 290 (Calories from Fat 160); Fat 18g (Saturated 7g); Cholesterol 70mg; Sodium 530mg; Carbohydrate 11g (Dietary Fiber 2g); Protein 23g.

Have a Minute?

For a festive touch, roll-up fresh flour tortillas and tie each with a long chive; serve on the side.

COME AND EAT!

Bored of regular old baked potatoes? Serve this steak with baked sweet potatoes topped with just a bit of butter and brown sugar.

Meat and Potato Skillet

4 SERVINGS

Have a Minute?

If you like a thicker gravy, coat the meat lightly with flour before browning.

COME AND EAT!

Serve with hot-from-the-oven buttermilk biscuits and, for dessert, chocolate chip cookies.

1 pound beef boneless sirloin
1 tablespoon vegetable oil
1 teaspoon garlic pepper
1 package (16 ounces) frozen green beans, potatoes, onions and red peppers
1 jar (12 ounces) beef gravy

1. Cut beef into thin strips (beef is easier to cut if partially frozen, about 1 1/2 hours). Heat oil and garlic pepper in 10-inch nonstick skillet over medium-high heat. Cook beef in oil, stirring occasionally, until brown.

2. Stir in vegetables and gravy; reduce heat to medium. Cover and simmer 7 to 9 minutes, stirring occasionally, until vegetables are crisp-tender.

1 Serving: Calories 245 (Calories from Fat 80); Fat 9g (Saturated 3g); Cholesterol 55mg; Sodium 520mg; Carbohydrate 19g (Dietary Fiber 3g); Protein 25g.

Ramen Beef and Vegetables

4 SERVINGS

Have a Minute?

Replace 2 tablespoons of the water with dry sherry for a nutty, delicate flavor.

COME AND EAT!

Serve with crisp egg rolls and sweet-and-sour sauce. For those who like it hot, mix together water and dry mustard for a very lively dipping sauce!

1 pound beef boneless sirloin
2 cups water
1 package (3 ounces) Oriental-flavor ramen soup mix
1 package (16 ounces) fresh stir-fry vegetables
1/4 cup stir-fry sauce

1. Cut beef into thin strips (beef is easier to cut if partially frozen, about 1 1/2 hours). Spray 12-inch nonstick skillet with cooking spray; heat over medium-high heat. Cook beef in skillet 3 to 5 minutes, stirring occasionally, until brown. Remove beef from skillet.

2. Heat water to boiling in same skillet. Break up noodles from soup mix into water; stir until slightly softened. Stir in vegetables.

3. Heat to boiling. Boil 5 to 7 minutes, stirring occasionally, until vegetables are crisp-tender. Stir in seasoning packet from soup mix, stir-fry sauce and beef. Cook 3 to 5 minutes, stirring frequently, until hot.

1 Serving: Calories 265 (Calories from Fat 80); Fat 9g (Saturated 3g); Cholesterol 55mg; Sodium 1270mg; Carbohydrate 25g (Dietary Fiber 4g); Protein 25g.

Mexican Steak Stir-Fry

4 SERVINGS

Kick up the flavor by using some chopped fresh jalapeño chile for a portion of the mild green bell pepper.

3/4 pound beef boneless sirloin

1 medium onion, chopped (1/2 cup)

1 small green bell pepper, chopped (1/2 cup)

1 clove garlic, finely chopped

1 cup frozen whole kernel corn

1/2 cup salsa

1 medium zucchini, sliced (2 cups)

1 can (15 to 16 ounces) pinto beans, rinsed and drained

1 can (14 1/2 ounces) whole tomatoes, undrained

1. Cut beef into 1/4 × 1/2-inch strips (beef is easier to cut if partially frozen, about 1 1/2 hours).

2. Spray 12-inch nonstick skillet or wok with cooking spray; heat over medium-high heat. Add beef, onion, bell pepper and garlic; stir-fry 4 to 5 minutes or until beef is brown.

3. Stir in remaining ingredients breaking up tomatoes. Cook about 5 minutes, stirring occasionally, until zucchini is tender and mixture is hot.

1 Serving: Calories 250 (Calories from Fat 25); Fat 3g (Saturated 1g); Cholesterol 40mg; Sodium 510mg; Carbohydrate 42g (Dietary Fiber 12g); Protein 26g.

Have a Minute?

For a final touch, sprinkle with shredded Monterey Jack cheese with jalapeño peppers.

COME AND EAT!

Serve with warm flour tortillas. For a nice change, stir enough sour cream into hot rice to make it creamy and then stir in canned green chilies.

Skillet Calzone

4 SERVINGS

Ground beef could be easily substituted for the beef sirloin strips.

Have a Minute?

Shaved fresh Parmesan cheese scattered over each serving adds a rich, tangy flavor.

COME AND EAT!

Spoon canned lemon pie filling into miniature graham cracker crusts (in individual foil tins); add a generous dollop of real whipped cream or nondairy whipped topping.

8 diagonally cut slices French bread, 1/2 inch thick

2 tablespoons grated Parmesan cheese

3/4 pound beef sirloin or flank steak, cut into thin strips

1 tablespoon olive or vegetable oil

1 small green bell pepper, sliced

1 or 2 cloves garlic, finely chopped

1 can (14 1/2 ounces) diced tomatoes with Italian-style herbs, undrained

1 can (8 ounces) pizza sauce

1 jar (4 1/2 ounces) sliced mushrooms, drained

1. Set oven control to broil. Place bread slices on ungreased cookie sheet. Spray bread with cooking spray; sprinkle with cheese. Broil with tops 4 to 6 inches from heat 1 to 2 minutes or until light brown; set aside.

2. Cut beef into thin strips (beef is easier to cut if partially frozen, about 1 1/2 hours). Heat oil in 10-inch nonstick skillet over medium-high heat. Cook beef, bell pepper and garlic in oil, stirring occasionally, until beef is brown.

3. Stir in tomatoes, pizza sauce and mushrooms. Cook 2 to 4 minutes or until hot. Place 2 toasted bread slices on each of 4 serving plates; top with beef mixture.

1 Serving: Calories 335 (Calories from Fat 100); Fat 11g (Saturated 3g); Cholesterol 45mg; Sodium 1020mg; Carbohydrate 39g (Dietary Fiber 4g); Protein 24g.

Beef Cubed Steaks with Mushroom-Cream Sauce

4 SERVINGS

For elegant entertaining, use 1/2-inch slices of beef tenderloin instead of cubed steak.

Have a Minute?

Stir in 1 to 2 teaspoons of prepared horseradish along with the sour cream in step 3.

COME AND EAT!

Serve over spinach fettuccine and a spinach salad tossed with crumbled bacon, mandarin orange segments and poppy seed dressing.

4 beef cubed steaks (4 ounces each)
1/2 teaspoon salt
1/2 teaspoon pepper
3 tablespoons vegetable oil
1 package (8 ounces) sliced mushrooms (3 cups)
1 cup sour cream with chives

1. Sprinkle both sides of beef steaks with salt and pepper. Heat 2 tablespoons of the oil in 10-inch nonstick skillet over medium-high heat. Cook beef in oil 5 to 6 minutes for medium doneness, turning once. Remove beef from skillet; keep warm.

2. Heat remaining 1 tablespoon oil and drippings in skillet over medium-high heat. Cook mushrooms in oil, stirring occasionally, until liquid evaporates; reduce heat to medium.

3. Stir in sour cream; cook until hot. Do not boil. Serve over beef.

1 Serving: Calories 395 (Calories from Fat 270); Fat 30g (Saturated 12g); Cholesterol 105mg; Sodium 370mg; Carbohydrate 5g (Dietary Fiber 1g); Protein 27g.

Black Bean and Beef Tostadas

6 SERVINGS

1/2 pound ground beef

1 medium onion, chopped (1/2 cup)

1 can (10 ounces) diced tomatoes and green chilies, undrained

1 can (15 ounces) black beans, rinsed and drained

6 tostada shells

1 cup shredded lettuce

2/3 cup chopped tomato

3/4 cup shredded Colby-Monterey Jack cheese (3 ounces)

1. Cook beef and onion in 10-inch skillet over medium heat 8 to 10 minutes, stirring occasionally, until beef is brown; drain. Stir in tomatoes. Heat to boiling; reduce heat to low. Simmer uncovered about 10 minutes or until liquid has evaporated. Stir in beans.

2. Heat tostada shells as directed on package. Top tostada shells with bean mixture, lettuce, tomato and cheese.

1 Serving: Calories 320 (Calories from Fat 135), Fat 15g (Saturated 7g); Cholesterol 40mg; Sodium 430mg; Carbohydrate 34g (Dietary Fiber 6g); Protein 18g.

Have a Minute?

This is such a neat little sauce—just mix sour cream with salsa and spoon over tostadas.

COME AND EAT!

For a sweet and sassy fruit salad, stir 1 tablespoon canned green chilies or fresh jalapeño pepper into a can of undrained fruit cocktail or tropical fruit blend.

Sloppy Joe Rotini

4 SERVINGS

1 pound ground beef

2 cups uncooked rotini pasta (6 ounces)

2 cups frozen whole kernel corn

1 cup water

1 small zucchini, sliced (1 cup)

1 jar (15 1/2 ounces) extra-thick-and-chunky sloppy joe sauce

1. Cook beef in 10-inch nonstick skillet over medium heat 8 to 10 minutes, stirring occasionally, until brown; drain. Stir in remaining ingredients.

2. Heat to boiling; reduce heat to medium. Cover and simmer about 15 minutes, stirring occasionally, until pasta is tender.

1 Serving: Calories 460 (Calories from Fat 155); Fat 17g (Saturated 7g); Cholesterol 65mg; Sodium 1170mg; Carbohydrate 52g (Dietary Fiber 3g); Protein 28g.

Have a Minute?

Sprinkle Cheddar cheese fish-shaped crackers over the casserole just before serving.

COME AND EAT!

Serve with thick slices of toast, carrot sticks and pickles.

Meatballs and Mashed Potatoes

4 SERVINGS

Purchasing frozen cooked meatballs eliminates the time needed to make your own meatballs. Use the added time to make a salad!

Have a Minute?

Try making homemade garlic mashed potatoes by adding 4 cut-up garlic cloves to the cooking water. Drain the water, but not the garlic, and mash potatoes with milk and butter.

COME AND EAT!

Some old-fashioned favorites just seem to hit the spot. So how about serving piping hot buttermilk biscuits or rolls, creamy coleslaw and, for dessert, apple pie a la mode.

2 cups water

1 container (8 ounces) au jus concentrate

3 tablespoons cornstarch

24 frozen cooked meatballs (about 1 1/2 inches in diameter)

1 small onion, sliced and separated into rings

1 small green bell pepper, cut into 1/4-inch strips

2 cups hot mashed potatoes

1. Mix water, au jus concentrate and cornstarch in 3-quart saucepan. Stir in meatballs, onion and bell pepper. Heat to boiling; reduce heat to medium. Cover and cook about 3 minutes, stirring occasionally, until vegetables are tender.

2. Serve meatballs over mashed potatoes.

1 Serving: Calories 750 (Calories from Fat 370); Fat 41g (Saturated 15g); Cholesterol 190mg; Sodium 1850mg; Carbohydrate 59g (Dietary Fiber 4g); Protein 40g.

Easy Stroganoff Meatballs

4 SERVINGS

Have a Minute?

Add 1 cup of frozen cut green beans with the meatballs in step 2.

COME AND EAT!

Ladle the meatballs with their creamy sauce over egg noodles, baked potatoes or rice.

1 1/4 cups beef broth

2 tablespoons all-purpose flour

2 teaspoons Worcestershire sauce

16 frozen cooked meatballs (about 1 1/2 inches in diameter)

1 jar (4 1/2 ounces) sliced mushrooms, drained

1/2 cup sour cream

1 tablespoon chopped fresh parsley

1. Beat broth, flour and Worcestershire sauce with wire whisk.

2. Place frozen meatballs and broth mixture in 10-inch skillet. Heat to boiling, stirring occasionally; reduce heat to low. Cover and simmer 4 to 6 minutes or until meatballs are hot.

3. Stir in mushrooms, sour cream and parsley; cook until hot. Do not boil.

1 Serving: Calories 395 (Calories from Fat 225); Fat 25g (Saturated 11g); Cholesterol 140mg; Sodium 1010mg; Carbohydrate 18g (Dietary Fiber 1g); Protein 26g.

Apple-Rosemary Pork and Rice

4 SERVINGS

The rice is cooked in apple juice instead of water for its subtle, sweet flavor.

1 1/2 cups apple juice

1 1/2 cups uncooked instant rice

2 tablespoons chopped fresh or 2 teaspoons crushed dried rosemary leaves

2 teaspoons vegetable oil

3/4 pound pork tenderloin, cut into 1/2-inch slices

1 medium onion, chopped (1/2 cup)

1 clove garlic, finely chopped

1/4 cup apple jelly

1 large unpeeled red cooking apple, sliced

Rosemary sprigs, if desired

1. Heat apple juice to boiling in 2-quart saucepan. Stir in rice and 1 tablespoon of the rosemary; remove from heat. Cover and let stand until ready to serve. Just before serving, fluff with fork.

2. Heat oil in 10-inch nonstick skillet over medium-high heat. Cook pork, onion, garlic and remaining 1 tablespoon rosemary in oil 6 to 8 minutes, stirring occasionally, until pork is slightly pink in center.

3. Stir in apple jelly and apple; cook until hot. Serve over rice. Garnish with rosemary sprigs.

1 Serving: Calories 370 (Calories from Fat 55); Fat 6g (Saturated 2g); Cholesterol 50mg; Sodium 50mg; Carbohydrate 63g (Dietary Fiber 6g); Protein 22g.

Have a Minute?

Experience the amazingly good flavor of toasted pecans or walnuts and sprinkle them on top of the pork and rice just before serving.

COME AND EAT!

Butternut, buttercup or acorn squash sprinkled with cinnamon and drizzled with honey would be a great accompaniment with this fall-inspired dish.

Nut-Crusted Pork Medallions

4 SERVINGS

The honey, cornmeal and pecans give the pork medallions a Southern flavor.

Have a Minute?

If you like sweet-and-hot and sweet-and-salty flavors, add a dash of hot pepper sauce to the honey and egg mixture in step 1.

COME AND EAT!

Add corn on the cob and baking powder biscuits to complete the meal.

1 egg

1/4 cup honey

3/4 to 1 pound pork tenderloin, cut into 1/2-inch slices

1 cup chopped pecans (4 ounces)

1/2 cup yellow cornmeal

1 teaspoon salt

1/2 teaspoon pepper

2 tablespoons vegetable oil

1. Mix egg and honey in small bowl. Add pork slices; toss to coat.

2. Place pecans, cornmeal, salt and pepper in food processor. Cover and process until finely chopped. Place pecan mixture in resealable plastic bag. Add pork slices; seal bag and shake to coat.

3. Heat oil in 10-inch nonstick skillet over medium-high heat. Cook pork in oil 6 to 8 minutes, turning once, until golden brown on outside and slightly pink in center.

1 Serving: Calories 515 (Calories from Fat 290); Fat 32g (Saturated 5g); Cholesterol 105mg; Sodium 55mg; Carbohydrate 37g (Dietary Fiber 3g); Protein 23g.

Caramelized Pork Slices

4 SERVINGS

Caramelizing meat adds a delicious, slightly sweet flavor.

1 pound pork tenderloin, cut into 1/2-inch slices

2 cloves garlic, finely chopped

2 tablespoons packed brown sugar

1 tablespoon orange juice

1 tablespoon molasses

1/2 teaspoon salt

1/4 teaspoon pepper

1. Spray 10-inch nonstick skillet with cooking spray; heat over medium-high heat.

2. Cook pork and garlic in skillet 6 to 8 minutes, turning occasionally, until pork is slightly pink in center. Drain if necessary.

3. Stir in remaining ingredients. Cook until mixture thickens and coats pork.

1 Serving: Calories 175 (Calories from Fat 35); Fat 4g (Saturated 1g); Cholesterol 65mg; Sodium 320mg; Carbohydrate 11g, (Dietary Fiber 0g); Protein 24g.

Have a Minute?

Slice a medium-sized onion and cook with pork and garlic in step 2.

COME AND EAT!

Serve with mashed sweet potatoes and a crisp green salad. Layer chocolate pudding with crumbled coconut macaroons in parfait glasses and top with whipped cream.

Chicken-Fried Pork

6 SERVINGS

This recipe cooks in a flash with the use of naturally thin-sliced pork cutlets!

COME AND EAT!

Serve with mashed potatoes, cooked collard greens or spinach and sliced ripe garden tomatoes.

1 1/2 pounds pork cutlets
1 tablespoon water
1 egg
1 cup saltine cracker crumbs (about 28 squares)
1/4 teaspoon pepper
1/4 cup vegetable oil
Milk Gravy (below)

1. If pork cutlets are large, cut into 6 serving pieces. Beat water and egg with wire whisk or hand beater. Mix cracker crumbs and pepper together. Dip pork into egg mixture, then coat with cracker crumbs.

2. Heat oil in 12-inch skillet over medium-high heat. Cook pork in oil 3 to 4 minutes, turning once, until brown on outside and slightly pink in center. Remove pork from skillet; keep warm.

3. Prepare Milk Gravy. Serve with pork.

MILK GRAVY

Vegetable oil
1/4 cup all-purpose flour
1/2 teaspoon salt
2 cups milk

Measure pork drippings; add enough oil to drippings, if necessary, to measure 1/4 cup. Return drippings to skillet. Stir in flour and salt. Cook over low heat, stirring constantly to loosen brown particles from skillet, until smooth and bubbly; remove from heat. Slowly pour milk into skillet, stirring constantly. Heat to boiling over low heat, stirring constantly. Boil and stir 1 minute.

1 Serving: Calories 375 (Calories from Fat 190); Fat 21g (Saturated 6g); Cholesterol 105mg; Sodium 440mg; Carbohydrate 17g (Dietary Fiber 0g); Protein 29g.

Pork Cutlets with Apple, Walnut and Gorgonzola Salsa

4 SERVINGS

Pumpkin pie spice is a combination of cinnamon, nutmeg, cloves and ginger.

1 tablespoon vegetable oil

3/4 teaspoon pumpkin pie spice

4 slices (3 to 4 ounces each) pork boneless loin, 1/4 inch thick

1 tablespoon orange juice

1/3 cup packed brown sugar

1/2 cup coarsely chopped walnuts, toasted*

2 medium red apples, coarsely chopped (2 cups)

1/4 cup crumbled Gorgonzola cheese

1. Heat oil in 10-inch nonstick skillet over medium-high heat. Stir 1/2 teaspoon of the pumpkin pie spice into oil. Cook pork in oil mixture 5 to 8 minutes, turning once, until slightly pink in center.

2. Mix the remaining 1/4 teaspoon pumpkin pie spice, the orange juice, brown sugar, walnuts, apples and cheese. Spoon over pork.

*To toast nuts, bake uncovered in ungreased shallow pan in 350° oven about 10 minutes, stirring occasionally, until golden brown. Or cook in ungreased heavy skillet over medium-low heat 5 to 7 minutes, stirring frequently until browning begins, then stirring constantly until golden brown.

1 Serving: Calories 410 (Calories from Fat 200); Fat 22g (Saturated 6g); Cholesterol 60mg; Sodium 160mg; Carbohydrate 32g (Dietary Fiber 2g); Protein 23g.

Have a Minute?

Add 1/2 teaspoon chopped fresh gingerroot to the salsa.

COME AND EAT!

This is especially good with sweet dumpling or acorn squash (which cooks in the microwave oven in just minutes) and sugar snap peas.

Speedy Pork Cacciatore

4 SERVINGS

Have a Minute?

Stir 1/4 cup sliced ripe olives into the sauce in step 3.

COME AND EAT!

For a great supper, pick up Italian bread and, for dessert, spumoni ice cream. Buon appetito!

8 ounces uncooked spaghetti

1 tablespoon olive or vegetable oil

1 pound pork boneless shoulder or sirloin, cut into 1-inch pieces

1 jar (28 ounces) primavera spaghetti sauce

1. Cook spaghetti and drain spaghetti as directed on package.

2. While spaghetti is cooking, heat oil in 10-inch nonstick skillet over medium-high heat. Cook pork in oil, stirring occasionally, until light brown.

3. Stir in spaghetti sauce. Heat to boiling; reduce heat to medium. Cover and cook about 5 minutes, stirring occasionally, until pork is slightly pink in center. Serve over spaghetti.

1 Serving: Calories 565 (Calories from Fat 190); Fat 21g (Saturated 5g); Cholesterol 75mg; Sodium 1390mg; Carbohydrate 64g (Dietary Fiber 5g); Protein 35g.

Thai Pork and Noodles

4 SERVINGS

The smooth and spicy peanut sauce complements the pork and noodles perfectly.

1 tablespoon vegetable oil

1 pound pork boneless shoulder or sirloin, cut into 1-inch cubes

2 cloves garlic, finely chopped

2 cups water

2 packages (3 ounces each) Oriental-flavor ramen soup mix

2 tablespoons creamy peanut butter

1 cup baby-cut carrots

1/2 teaspoon crushed red pepper

1 medium zucchini, cut in half and sliced (1 cup)

1. Heat oil in 10-inch nonstick skillet over medium-high heat. Cook pork and garlic in oil, stirring occasionally, until pork is brown.

2. Stir in water, seasoning packets from soup mixes, peanut butter, carrots and red pepper. Heat to boiling; reduce heat to medium. Cover and cook 5 to 6 minutes or until carrots are crisp-tender.

3. Gently break each block of noodles in half. Add noodles and zucchini to skillet. Heat to boiling. Boil uncovered 1 minute, stirring occasionally to separate noodles, until noodles are soft.

1 Serving: Calories 420 (Calories from Fat 190); Fat 21g (Saturated 6g); Cholesterol 50mg; Sodium 1060mg; Carbohydrate 35g (Dietary Fiber 3g); Protein 26g.

Have a Minute?

Sprinkle the noodles with sliced green onions and chopped peanuts.

COME AND EAT!

Serve with sliced cucumbers splashed with seasoned rice wine vinegar and red pepper flakes.

Grilled Honey-Mustard Pork Chops

4 SERVINGS

The sweet honey glaze on these chops browns easily, so watch the chops carefully.

Have a Minute?

Stir in mustard seeds for extra flavor and crunch in step 2.

COME AND EAT!

Potato salad and marinated vegetables, usually available at the deli, are easy to plan for. Cool, juicy watermelon slices provide a simple, but delicious, dessert.

1/4 cup honey

2 tablespoons Dijon mustard

1 tablespoon orange juice

1 teaspoon chopped fresh or 1/4 teaspoon dried tarragon leaves

1 teaspoon cider vinegar

1/2 teaspoon white Worcestershire sauce

Dash of onion powder

4 pork butterfly loin chops, 1 inch thick (about 1 pound)

1. Heat coals or gas grill.

2. Mix all ingredients except pork.

3. Cover and grill pork 4 to 6 inches from medium heat 14 to 16 minutes, brushing occasionally with honey mixture and turning once, until pork is tender and slightly pink in center. Discard any remaining honey mixture.

1 Serving: Calories 220 (Calories from Fat 65); Fat 7g (Saturated 3g); Cholesterol 55mg; Sodium 140mg; Carbohydrate 19g (Dietary Fiber 0g); Protein 20g.

Greek Honey and Lemon Pork Chops

4 SERVINGS

Greek seasoning, located in the spice aisle of your supermarket includes salt, pepper, garlic, MSG, oregano, parsley and beef flavor.

4 pork loin chops or ribs, 1/2 inch thick (about 1 pound)

1 tablespoon all-purpose Greek seasoning

1 teaspoon grated lemon peel

2 tablespoons lemon juice

3 tablespoons honey

1. Set oven control to broil. Place pork on rack in broiler pan.

2. Mix remaining ingredients. Brush honey mixture evenly on tops of pork chops.

3. Broil with tops 4 to 6 inches from heat 7 to 8 minutes, turning once and brushing with honey mixture, until slightly pink when cut near bone. Discard any remaining honey mixture.

1 Serving: Calories 220 (Calories from Fat 70); Fat 8g (Saturated 3g); Cholesterol 65mg; Sodium 40mg; Carbohydrate 14g (Dietary Fiber 0g); Protein 23g.

Have a Minute?

Add chopped fresh oregano to honey mixture for authentic Greek flavor.

COME AND EAT!

Prepare a salad using fresh spinach, artichoke hearts, tomatoes and ripe olives for a Mediterranean-inspired salad.

Honey-Mustard Ham

4 SERVINGS

No honey mustard on hand? Just mix 1 tablespoon of honey with two tablespoons of Dijon mustard for a quick homemade substitute.

1 pound fully cooked ham slice, about 1 inch thick

1/4 cup water

3 tablespoons honey mustard

1/2 cup sour cream

1 medium green onion, sliced (2 tablespoons)

1. Cut ham into 4 serving pieces. Mix water and honey mustard in 10-inch skillet. Add ham.

2. Cover and heat to boiling; reduce heat to low. Simmer about 15 minutes, turning ham once, until ham is hot. Remove ham from skillet; keep warm.

3. Stir sour cream into mixture in skillet; heat 1 minute. Pour over ham. Sprinkle with onion.

1 Serving: Calories 260 (Calories from Fat 145); Fat 16g (Saturated 7g); Cholesterol 85mg; Sodium 1860mg; Carbohydrate 2g (Dietary Fiber 0g); Protein 27g.

Have a Minute?

Add 2 cans whole potatoes (drained) to skillet in step 1 with ham.

COME AND EAT!

Serve with sautéed zucchini, peas or broccoli.

Honey-Mustard Ham

Skillet Ham and Vegetables Au Gratin

6 SERVINGS

A gratin is any dish that is topped with cheese; au gratin applies to any dish prepared this way. Although gratins are typically baked, preparing your gratin in a skillet gives you the same delicious results but in a fraction of the time.

1 tablespoon vegetable oil

1 1/2 cups cut-up fully cooked ham

1 large onion, chopped (1 cup)

1 package (5.25 ounces) au gratin potato mix

2 1/2 cups hot water

1/4 teaspoon pepper

1 package (16 ounces) frozen broccoli, cauliflower and carrots, thawed

1 cup shredded Cheddar cheese (4 ounces)

1. Heat oil in 10-inch skillet over medium-high heat. Cook ham and onion in oil about 5 minutes, stirring frequently, until onion is tender.

2. Stir in potatoes, sauce mix from potato mix, hot water and pepper. Heat to boiling; reduce heat to low. Cover and simmer 10 minutes, stirring occasionally.

3. Stir in vegetables. Cover and simmer about 10 minutes or until potatoes are tender. Sprinkle with cheese.

1 Serving: Calories 290 (Calories from Fat 115); Fat 12g (Saturated 6g); Cholesterol 35mg; Sodium 1075mg; Carbohydrate 29g (Dietary Fiber 3g); Protein 17g.

Have a Minute?

Stir a 4 ounce can of diced green chilies, or a 2-ounce jar of diced pimiento (drained) into the potatoes in step 2.

COME AND EAT!

Cut six, 1-inch slices of iceberg lettuce and top with chopped tomatoes for a simple salad.

Skillet Ham and Vegetables Au Gratin

MEATLESS AND MARVELOUS

Sautéed Bean Cakes with
Tomato Salsa (page 66)

Crunchy Bean Skillet

6 SERVINGS

You won't miss the meat in this hearty one-dish meal.

Have a Minute?

For added flavor, toast the walnuts in a skillet over medium-low heat for about 5 to 7 minutes, stirring frequently, until light brown.

COME AND EAT!

Serve over hot cooked pasta, or serve with a great chewy or crusty bread.

3 cans (15 to 16 ounces each) cannellini beans, rinsed and drained

1 jar (14 ounces) spaghetti sauce

2 medium stalks celery, sliced (1 cup)

4 medium green onions, sliced (1/2 cup)

1 tablespoon chopped fresh parsley or 1 teaspoon dried parsley flakes

1 tablespoon chopped fresh or 1 teaspoon dried basil leaves

2 teaspoons chopped fresh or 1/2 teaspoon dried oregano leaves

1 cup shredded mozzarella cheese (4 ounces)

1/2 cup coarsely chopped walnuts

1. Mix all ingredients except cheese and walnuts in 10-inch skillet.

2. Heat to boiling; reduce heat to low. Sprinkle with cheese.

3. Cover and simmer 3 to 5 minutes or just until cheese is melted. Sprinkle with walnuts.

1 Serving: Calories 200 (Calories from Fat 110); Fat 12g (Saturated 3g); Cholesterol 10mg; Sodium 1030mg; Carbohydrate 18g (Dietary Fiber 5g); Protein 10g.

Black Bean Enchiladas

4 SERVINGS

Regular refried beans can be substituted for refried black beans.

1 teaspoon vegetable oil

1 medium onion, chopped (1/2 cup)

1 clove garlic, crushed

1 cup sour cream

1 tablespoon lime juice

1/2 teaspoon ground cumin

2 cans (16 ounces each) refried black beans

8 whole wheat or regular flour tortillas (8 to 10 inches in diameter)

1 can (15 ounces) tomato sauce

1/2 cup shredded Monterey Jack cheese with jalapeño peppers (2 ounces)

1. Heat oil in 10-inch skillet over medium-high heat. Cook onion and garlic in oil about 2 minutes, stirring occasionally, until onion is crisp-tender. Stir in sour cream, lime juice, cumin and beans.

2. Spoon about 1/3 cup bean mixture onto each tortilla. Roll tortillas around filling; place seam sides down in skillet. Pour tomato sauce over tortillas. Sprinkle with cheese. Cook over low heat 10 to 15 minutes or until hot and bubbly.

1 Serving: Calories 570 (Calories from Fat 180); Fat 20g (Saturated 11g); Cholesterol 50mg; Sodium 1500mg; Carbohydrate 90g (Dietary Fiber 20g); Protein 28g.

Have a Minute?

Place sprigs of fresh cilantro on flour tortillas before spooning each with bean mixture.

COME AND EAT!

Add a crunchy salad of shredded carrots and jicama tossed with a little oil, cumin, salt and pepper.

Sautéed Bean Cakes with Tomato Salsa

6 SERVINGS

Have a Minute?

These patties are tasty all on their own, but are terrific served in hamburger buns with additional salsa and lettuce.

COME AND EAT!

Serve with corn or flavored tortilla chips.

4 cups fine soft whole wheat or white bread crumbs (about 6 slices bread)

1/2 cup chopped fresh parsley

1/2 cup plain fat-free or regular yogurt

1 tablespoon Dijon mustard

1 tablespoon lemon juice

2 medium green onions, finely chopped (2 tablespoons)

2 egg whites, beaten

2 cans (15 to 16 ounces each) great northern beans, rinsed, drained and mashed

2 tablespoons margarine or butter

1 jar (8 ounces) salsa (1 cup)

1. Mix 3 1/2 cups of the bread crumbs, parsley, yogurt, mustard, lemon juice, onions, egg whites and beans. Shape mixture into 12 patties. Coat patties with remaining bread crumbs.

2. Melt margarine in 10-inch nonstick skillet over medium heat. Cook patties in margarine 5 to 6 minutes, turning after 3 minutes, until golden brown. Serve with salsa.

1 Serving: Calories 260 (Calories from Fat 25); Fat 3g (Saturated 1g); Cholesterol 0mg; Sodium 630mg; Carbohydrate 50g (Dietary Fiber 10g); Protein 18g.

Cajun Bean Patties

4 SERVINGS

Try using black-eyed peas in place of the kidney beans for a change of pace.

**2 cans (15 to 16 ounces each) dark red kidney beans, rinsed and
drained**

1 egg

1/4 cup unseasoned dry bread crumbs

2 teaspoons Cajun or Creole seasoning

1 tablespoon vegetable oil

Sour cream, if desired

1. Mash beans, egg, bread crumbs and Cajun seasoning. Shape mixture into 4 patties, 1/2 inch thick, using wet hands.

2. Heat oil in 10-inch skillet over medium-high heat. Cook patties in oil 6 to 8 minutes, turning once, until hot. Serve with sour cream.

1 Serving: Calories 215 (Calories from Fat 55); Fat 6g (Saturated 1g); Cholesterol 55mg; Sodium 710mg; Carbohydrate 35g (Dietary Fiber 8g); Protein 13g

Have a Minute?

Want a little more zing? Add about 1/4 cup chopped pickled okra to the bean mixture.

COME AND EAT!

Make an easy rice side dish by using a packet of Spanish rice mix.

Vegetarian Fried Rice

4 SERVINGS

If you're in the mood for a lighter meal, this meatless main dish is perfect!

Have a Minute?

Stir in a can of baby corn cobs or nuggets (drained), with the pea pods in step 3.

COME AND EAT!

For an easy, cooling dessert, toss canned mandarin orange segments (drained) with chopped crystallized ginger and spoon over orange or pineapple sherbet.

2 1/4 cups water

2 1/2 cups uncooked instant brown rice

2 eggs, beaten

1 tablespoon vegetable oil

2 medium carrots, sliced (1 cup)

4 medium green onions, sliced (1/2 cup)

1 clove garlic, finely chopped

2 cups Chinese pea pods, cut in half

1 cup bean sprouts

2 tablespoons soy sauce

1. Heat water to boiling in 2-quart saucepan; stir in rice. Heat to boiling; reduce heat to low. Cover and simmer 5 minutes. Remove from heat. Stir rice; cover and let stand 5 minutes. Fluff with fork.

2. While rice is cooking, spray 10-inch nonstick skillet with cooking spray; heat over medium heat. Cook eggs in skillet until firm; remove from skillet. When eggs are cool, cut into small pieces.

3. Heat oil in same skillet over medium-high heat. Cook carrots, onions and garlic in oil 1 minute. Stir in pea pods and bean sprouts. Cook 2 minutes, stirring occasionally. Stir in rice, soy sauce and eggs. Cook, stirring occasionally, until hot.

1 Serving: Calories 255 (Calories from Fat 65); Fat 7g (Saturated 2g); Cholesterol 105mg; Sodium 570mg; Carbohydrate 43g (Dietary Fiber 5g); Protein 10g.

Thai Noodles with Peanut Sauce

4 SERVINGS

To speed preparation, look for bottled peanut sauce in the Oriental section of the grocery store. Use about 2/3 to 3/4 cup purchased peanut sauce in place of the peanut butter, soy sauce, gingerroot, crushed red pepper and chicken broth.

1/2 cup creamy peanut butter

2 tablespoons soy sauce

1 teaspoon grated gingerroot

1/2 teaspoon crushed red pepper

1/2 cup vegetable or chicken broth

8 ounces uncooked rice stick noodles

1 cup bean sprouts

1 medium red bell pepper, cut lengthwise into fourths then crosswise into thin slices

2 medium green onions, sliced (1/4 cup)

2 tablespoons chopped fresh cilantro, if desired

1. Mix peanut butter, soy sauce, gingerroot and red pepper until smooth in small bowl. Gradually stir in broth.

2. Heat 2 quarts water to boiling. Break noodles in half and pull apart slightly while dropping into boiling water. Cook uncovered 1 minute; drain.

3. Place noodles in large bowl. Add peanut butter mixture, bean sprouts, bell pepper and onions; toss. Sprinkle with cilantro.

1 Serving: Calories 345 (Calories from Fat 155); Fat 17g (Saturated 4g); Cholesterol 0mg; Sodium 790mg; Carbohydrate 40g (Dietary Fiber 3g); Protein 11g.

Have a Minute?

Sprinkle toasted coconut along with the cilantro in step 3 for a great Thai flavor accent.

COME AND EAT!

Serve creamy lemon or mango sorbet with old-fashioned ice cream wafer cookies for dessert.

Noodles Romanoff

6 SERVINGS

Yes, a lighter version of this very rich combination can be made by using low-fat or fat-free sour cream and fat-free grated Parmesan cheese. Reduced-calorie vegetable oil spread could take the place of margarine or butter.

Have a Minute?

If you love that smoky bacon flavor of car-bonara, but don't want the meat, add 1/4 cup imitation bacon bits in step 2.

COME AND EAT!

Sauté a 16-ounce bag of frozen bell pepper and onion stir-fry and add a raspberry salad or Caesar salad from a complete bagged salad kit.

4 cups uncooked wide egg noodles (8 ounces)

2 cups sour cream

1/2 cup grated Parmesan cheese

1 tablespoon chopped fresh chives

1 teaspoon salt

1/8 teaspoon pepper

1 large clove garlic, crushed

2 tablespoons margarine or butter

1. Cook and drain noodles as directed on package.

2. While noodles are cooking, mix sour cream, 1/4 cup of the cheese, the chives, salt, pepper and garlic.

3. Place noodles in large bowl. Stir in margarine. Fold in sour cream mixture. Place noodles on warm platter. Sprinkle with remaining 1/4 cup cheese. Serve immediately.

1 Serving: Calories 310 (Calories from Fat 115); Fat 13g (Saturated 6g); Cholesterol 65mg; Sodium 640mg; Carbohydrate 36g (Dietary Fiber 1g); Protein 13g.

Polenta with Vegetable Marinara Sauce

4 SERVINGS

Use shredded fresh Parmesan, Asiago or Romano cheese instead of mozzarella if you prefer a sharper, more tangy flavor.

1 cup yellow cornmeal

3/4 cup cold water

2 1/2 cups boiling water

1/2 teaspoon salt

1 cup shredded mozzarella cheese (4 ounces)

1 tablespoon olive or vegetable oil

1 package (8 ounces) sliced mushrooms (3 cups)

1 medium zucchini, cut lengthwise in half then crosswise into slices (2 cups)

1 medium onion, chopped (1/2 cup)

1 clove garlic, finely chopped

1 jar (28 ounces) spaghetti sauce

Shredded Parmesan cheese, if desired

Have a Minute?

Scatter fresh basil, oregano and rosemary leaves over the Parmesan cheese.

COME AND EAT!

Serve a salad made with frisée lettuce and arugula splashed with vinaigrette and a twist of freshly ground pepper.

1. Mix cornmeal and cold water in 2-quart saucepan. Stir in boiling water and salt. Cook, over medium-high heat, stirring constantly, until mixture thickens and boils; reduce heat to low. Cover and cook 10 minutes, stirring occasionally. Stir in mozzarella cheese until smooth; keep polenta warm.

2. While polenta is cooking, heat oil in 10-inch nonstick skillet over medium-high heat. Cook mushrooms, zucchini, onion and garlic in oil 6 to 7 minutes, stirring occasionally, until tender. Stir in spaghetti sauce; cook until hot.

3. Spoon polenta evenly over center of individual dinner plates or serving platter. Spoon sauce over polenta. Sprinkle with Parmesan cheese.

1 Serving: Calories 415 (Calories from Fat 160); Fat 18g (Saturated 5g); Cholesterol 15mg; Sodium 1940mg; Carbohydrate 53g (Dietary Fiber 7g); Protein 17g.

Polenta with Italian Vegetables

6 SERVINGS

Polenta is a thick, creamy Italian dish that also may be called cornmeal mush.

Have a Minute?

If company is coming, stir in 1 tablespoon small-sized capers in step 3 and pass a bowl of the freshly shredded cheese.

COME AND EAT!

Serve with rustic, crusty bread and a fruity, extra-virgin olive oil for dipping.

1 cup yellow cornmeal

3/4 cup cold water

2 1/2 cups boiling water

1/2 teaspoon salt

2/3 cup shredded Swiss cheese (2 1/2 ounces)

2 teaspoons olive or vegetable oil

2 medium zucchini or yellow summer squash, sliced (3 cups)

1 medium red bell pepper, chopped (1 cup)

1 small onion, chopped (1/4 cup)

1 clove garlic, crushed

1/4 cup chopped fresh or 1 tablespoon dried basil leaves

1 can (14 ounces) artichoke heart quarters, drained

1. Mix cornmeal and cold water in 2-quart saucepan. Stir in boiling water and salt. Cook, stirring constantly, until mixture thickens and boils; reduce heat to low. Cover and simmer 10 minutes, stirring occasionally. Add cheese and stir until smooth; keep polenta warm.

2. While polenta is cooking, heat oil in 10-inch skillet over medium-high heat. Cook zucchini, bell pepper, onion and garlic in oil about 5 minutes, stirring occasionally, until vegetables are crisp-tender.

3. Stir in basil and artichoke hearts. Serve vegetable mixture over polenta.

1 Serving: Calories 170 (Calories from Fat 45); Fat 5g (Saturated 3g); Cholesterol 10mg; Sodium 390mg; Carbohydrate 29g (Dietary Fiber 6g); Protein 8g.

Cornmeal Pancakes with Spicy Chili Topping

8 PANCAKES

Make a double batch of pancakes and freeze one-half for spur-of-the-moment meals.

Have a Minute?

Corn lovers can add 1/2 cup thawed frozen corn to the pancake bater.

COME AND EAT!

Sour cream and chopped green onions would be great with these hearty pancakes.

3/4 cup Bisquick Original baking mix

1/2 cup yellow cornmeal

1 cup milk

1 egg

1 cup shredded sharp Cheddar cheese (4 ounces)

1 can (15 to 16 ounces) spicy chili beans, undrained

3/4 cup thick-and-chunky salsa

1/2 cup frozen whole kernel corn

1. Heat griddle or skillet over medium heat or to 375°. Grease with margarine if necessary. Beat baking mix, cornmeal, milk and egg with wire whisk or hand beater in medium bowl until well blended. Stir in cheese.

2. Pour batter by 1/4 cupfuls onto hot griddle. Cook until edges are dry. Turn; cook until golden.

3. While pancakes are cooking, mix beans, salsa and corn in 2-quart saucepan. Cook over medium heat about 5 minutes, stirring occasionally, until hot. Top pancakes with bean mixture.

1 Pancake: Calories 395 (Calories from Fat 145); Fat 16g (Saturated 8g); Cholesterol 85mg; Sodium 1050mg; Carbohydrate 50g (Dietary Fiber 6g); Protein 19g.

Cornmeal Pancakes with Spicy Chili Topping

Baked Potato Primavera

4 SERVINGS

For variety, try frozen potato patties that are warmed in the toaster.

┌─*Have a Minute?*─┐

*Want dressier potatoes?
Sprinkle vegetable mix-
ture with chopped,
oil-packed sun-dried
tomatoes.*

COME AND EAT!

Tira Mi Su couldn't be an easier dessert—fill sponge cake cups with ready-to-eat vanilla pudding and sprinkle with cocoa. If you'd like, drizzle a little rum on the sponge cake before filling with pudding.

4 baking potatoes

1/2 cup water

1 package (16 ounces) frozen broccoli, carrots and cauliflower

1 container (5 ounces) garlic- and herb-flavored soft spreadable cheese

1. Pierce potatoes to allow steam to escape. Arrange about 1 inch apart in circle on microwavable paper towel. Microwave uncovered on High 10 to 12 minutes or until tender.

2. While potatoes are cooking, heat water to boiling in 2-quart saucepan. Stir in vegetables; reduce heat to medium. Cover and simmer 3 to 7 minutes, stirring occasionally, until tender; drain.

3. Stir cheese into vegetables until melted. Spoon over baked potatoes.

1 Serving: Calories 330 (Calories from Fat 110); Fat 12g (Saturated 8g); Cholesterol 35mg; Sodium 130mg; Carbohydrate 53g (Dietary Fiber 7g); Protein 9g.

Crusted Chile-Potato Cakes

6 SERVINGS

Leftover mashed potatoes or instant mashed potatoes also could be used for this recipe.

1 package (20 ounces) refrigerated mashed potatoes (2 2/3 cups)
1 cup frozen whole kernel corn
1 cup shredded Cheddar cheese (4 ounces)
1 can (4 ounces) chopped green chilies, drained
3 tablespoons yellow cornmeal
2 tablespoons vegetable oil
1/2 cup salsa

1. Mix potatoes, corn, cheese and chilies. Shape mixture into six 4-inch patties. Coat patties with cornmeal.

2. Heat oil in 12-inch nonstick skillet over medium-high heat. Cook patties in oil 6 to 7 minutes, carefully turning once, until golden brown. Serve with salsa.

1 Serving: Calories 255 (Calories from Fat 110); Fat 12g (Saturated 5g); Cholesterol 20mg; Sodium 480mg; Carbohydrate 31g (Dietary Fiber 2g); Protein 8g.

Have a Minute?

Stir in 2 tablespoons canned chopped ripe olives in step 1.

COME AND EAT!

Serve with grilled zucchini or yellow summer squash that's been brushed with a mixture of oil and chili powder.

Seasoned Potato and Spinach Frittata

4 SERVINGS

Another way to serve a frittata is to cut a loaf of focaccia bread horizontally in half; place frittata between bread halves and cut into wedges.

Have a Minute?

Stir in chopped roasted red or fresh red bell pepper in step 1.

COME AND EAT!

Serve with vegetarian breakfast sausage links or patties.

1 tablespoon vegetable oil

2 cups frozen country-style seasoned potato wedges with skin

6 eggs

1/4 cup milk

2 cups frozen cut leaf spinach (from 16-ounce package), thawed and squeezed to drain

1/2 cup shredded Cheddar cheese (2 ounces)

1/4 teaspoon salt

1. Heat oil in 10-inch nonstick skillet over medium-high heat. Cook potatoes in oil 2 minutes, turning occasionally.

2. Beat eggs with wire whisk or hand beater in medium bowl. Stir in milk, spinach, cheese and salt. Pour egg mixture over potatoes in skillet; reduce heat to low. Cover and simmer 10 to 12 minutes or until set in center. Cut into wedges.

1 Serving: Calories 310 (Calories from Fat 180); Fat 20g (Saturated 7g); Cholesterol 330mg; Sodium 750mg; Carbohydrate 20g (Dietary Fiber 4g); Protein 17g.

Seasoned Potato and Spinach Frittata

Curried Potato and Garden Vegetable Sauce

4 SERVINGS

Have a Minute?

Crushed red pepper added in step 1 will fire up the flavor and the heat quotient.

COME AND EAT!

Raisins, chopped hard-cooked eggs, cashews or peanuts, sliced green onions and plain yogurt would be tasty toppings to have at the table.

1/2 cup water

1 package (16 ounces) frozen sweet peas, potatoes and carrots

3/4 cup milk

1 1/2 to 2 teaspoons curry powder

1/4 teaspoon salt

1 medium zucchini, cut lengthwise in half then crosswise into slices (2 cups)

1 medium tomato, seeded and chopped (3/4 cup)

1 can (10 3/4 ounces) condensed cream of potato soup

2 cups hot cooked couscous or rice

1. Heat water to boiling in 3-quart saucepan. Stir in frozen vegetables. Heat to boiling; reduce heat to low. Cover and simmer 6 to 8 minutes, stirring occasionally, until crisp-tender.

2. Stir in remaining ingredients except couscous. Simmer uncovered 2 to 4 minutes, stirring occasionally, until zucchini is tender and mixture is hot. Serve over couscous.

1 Serving: Calories 170 (Calories from Fat 25); Fat 3g (Saturated 2g); Cholesterol 10mg; Sodium 770mg; Carbohydrate 35g (Dietary Fiber 6g); Protein 7g.

Curried Potato and Garden Vegetable Sauce

Middle East Vegetable Tacos

6 SERVINGS

The vegetable mixture would also taste great served over strands of spaghetti squash or pasta.

—*Have a Minute?*—

Kalamata olives added to the vegetable mixture will add a nice salty tang.

COME AND EAT!

Serve with hot cooked couscous that has been cooked in chicken broth and olive oil; toss with grated lemon peel.

1 tablespoon olive or vegetable oil

1 medium eggplant (1 pound), cut into 1/2-inch cubes

1 medium red bell pepper, cut into 1/2-inch strips

1 medium onion, cut into 1/2-inch wedges

1 can (14 1/2 ounces) diced tomatoes with roasted garlic, onion and oregano, undrained

1/4 teaspoon salt

1 container (8 ounces) refrigerated hummus

12 taco shells

Plain yogurt or sour cream, if desired

1. Heat oil in 10-inch nonstick skillet over medium-high heat. Cook eggplant, bell pepper and onion in oil 5 to 7 minutes, stirring occasionally, until vegetables are crisp-tender.

2. Stir in tomatoes and salt; reduce heat to medium. Cover and cook about 5 minutes or until eggplant is tender.

3. Spread scant 2 tablespoons hummus on half of inside of each taco shell. Spoon about 1/2 cup vegetable mixture over hummus in each shell. Serve with yogurt.

1 Serving: Calories 255 (Calories from Fat 110); Fat 12g (Saturated 2g); Cholesterol 0mg; Sodium 550mg; Carbohydrate 38g (Dietary Fiber 7g); Protein 6g.

Easy Skillet Eggplant Lasagna

4 SERVINGS

Eggplant has been called "the vegetarian's beef" because of its meaty texture and its ability to take on the flavors of ingredients that accompany it.

1 egg

1 medium eggplant (1 pound), cut into eight 1/2-inch slices

1/2 cup seasoned dry bread crumbs

2 tablespoons vegetable oil

1 jar (14 ounces) spaghetti sauce

1 cup shredded mozzarella cheese (4 ounces)

1. Beat egg slightly in pie plate or shallow bowl. Dip eggplant slices into egg, then coat with bread crumbs.

2. Heat oil in 12-inch nonstick skillet over medium heat. Cook eggplant in oil 2 to 4 minutes, turning once, until golden brown.

3. Pour spaghetti sauce over eggplant; sprinkle with cheese. Heat to boiling; reduce heat to medium. Cover and cook 3 to 4 minutes or until eggplant is tender and hot.

1 Serving: Calories 310 (Calories from Fat 160); Fat 18g (Saturated 6g); Cholesterol 70mg; Sodium 960mg; Carbohydrate 29g (Dietary Fiber 5g); Protein 13g.

Have a Minute?

Add 1 tablespoon chopped fresh basil to the bread crumbs.

COME AND EAT!

All that's needed to complete the meal is toasted French bread and a small tossed salad.

Moroccan-Spiced Vegetables and Couscous

4 SERVINGS

Wake up your taste buds with this skillet supper. The Moroccan spice combination of cumin and cinnamon added to sweet potatoes, spinach and couscous makes a lively but easy one-dish meal.

Have a Minute?

Fresh tomato blends very well with Moroccan flavors; chop 1 large tomato and add in step 2.

COME AND EAT!

Serve with pita bread and plain yogurt mixed with chopped cucumber.

1 tablespoon olive or vegetable oil

1 large onion, chopped (1 cup)

2 cloves garlic, finely chopped

2 cups frozen cut leaf spinach (from 16-ounce package), thawed and squeezed to drain

1/2 cup raisins

1 teaspoon ground cumin

1/2 teaspoon ground cinnamon

1/2 teaspoon salt

1 can (14 1/2 ounces) chicken broth

1 can (23 ounces) sweet potatoes, cut into pieces

1 cup uncooked couscous

1. Heat oil in 10-inch skillet over medium-high heat. Cook onion and garlic in oil 2 to 3 minutes, stirring occasionally, until onion is tender.

2. Stir in remaining ingredients except couscous; heat to boiling.

3. Stir in couscous; remove from heat. Cover and let stand about 5 minutes or until liquid is absorbed.

1 Serving: Calories 485 (Calories from Fat 55); Fat 6g (Saturated 1g); Cholesterol 0mg; Sodium 1280mg; Carbohydrate 100g (Dietary Fiber 7g); Protein 15g.

Portobello Mushroom Fajita

6 SERVINGS

You will never miss the meat in these fajitas because portobello mushrooms have a flavorful, meaty texture.

1 tablespoon vegetable oil

1 clove garlic, finely chopped

1 teaspoon ground cumin

1/2 teaspoon salt

3/4 pound fresh portobello mushrooms, thinly sliced (6 cups)

2 cups frozen stir-fry bell peppers and onions (from 16-ounce package)

1/4 cup chopped fresh cilantro

2 tablespoons lime juice

6 flour tortillas (8 to 10 inches in diameter)

Guacamole or sour cream, if desired

Salsa, if desired

1. Heat oil, garlic, cumin and salt in 10-inch nonstick skillet over medium-high heat. Cook mushrooms and bell pepper mixture in oil 5 to 7 minutes, stirring frequently, until vegetables are crisp-tender. Sprinkle with cilantro and lime juice.

2. Spoon about 1/2 cup mushroom mixture onto each tortilla; roll up. Serve with guacamole and salsa.

1 Serving: Calories 180 (Calories from Fat 55); Fat 6g (Saturated 1g); Cholesterol 0mg; Sodium 400mg; Carbohydrate 29g (Dietary Fiber 2g); Protein 5g.

Have a Minute?

Sprinkle shredded white Cheddar cheese over mushroom mixture before rolling up in tortilla.

COME AND EAT!

For a refreshing and light dessert, arrange jarred mango slices and sliced kiwi fruit on a serving platter or individual serving plates. Drizzle with a mixture of equal parts honey and frozen limeade (thawed).

4

No-Fuss Pasta and Pizza

Chili Beef 'n' Noodles (page 94)

Fiesta Pork with Southwestern Cream Sauce

4 SERVINGS

This recipe also can be prepared using one pound skinless, boneless chicken breast, cut into one-inch pieces.

Have a Minute?

For a real flavor kick, stir in 1 to 2 teaspoons of chopped canned chipotle chilies in adobo sauce in step 3.

COME AND EAT!

Serve with corn bread sticks or muffins and whipped butter mixed with chopped black olives.

1 package (9 ounces) refrigerated uncooked angel hair pasta

1 tablespoon vegetable oil

1 teaspoon ground cumin

1 teaspoon chili powder

1 pound pork tenderloin, cut into 1/2-inch slices

1 cup whipping (heavy) cream

1 can (11 ounces) whole kernel corn with red and green peppers, drained

1/2 cup thick-and-chunky salsa

1. Cook and drain pasta as directed on package.

2. While pasta is cooking, heat oil, cumin and chili powder in 12-inch nonstick skillet over medium-high heat. Cook pork in oil mixture, turning once, until brown.

3. Stir in whipping cream. Cook 5 minutes, stirring occasionally. Stir in corn and salsa. Cook until hot. Serve over pasta.

1 Serving: Calories 655 (Calories from Fat 250); Fat 28g (Saturated 14g); Cholesterol 135mg; Sodium 410mg; Carbohydrate 69g (Dietary Fiber 4g); Protein 36g.

Linguine with Tuscan Vegetable Alfredo Sauce

4 SERVINGS

The beans in this meatless pasta dish make it surprisingly hearty.

1 package (9 ounces) refrigerated uncooked linguine or fettuccine

1 tablespoon olive or vegetable oil

1 medium zucchini, sliced (2 cups)

12 baby-cut carrots, cut lengthwise in half

1 package (8 ounces) sliced mushrooms (3 cups)

1 clove garlic, finely chopped

3/4 teaspoon dried thyme leaves

1 container (10 ounces) refrigerated Alfredo sauce

1 can (15 to 16 ounces) cannellini beans, rinsed and drained

1. Cook and drain linguine as directed on package.

2. While linguine is cooking, heat oil in 12-inch nonstick skillet over medium-high heat. Cook zucchini, carrots, mushrooms, garlic and thyme in oil 5 to 7 minutes, stirring occasionally, until vegetables are tender.

3. Stir in Alfredo sauce and beans. Cook, stirring occasionally, until thoroughly heated. Serve over linguine.

1 Serving: Calories 680 (Calories from Fat 270; Fat 30g (Saturated 12g); Cholesterol 50mg; Sodium 880mg; Carbohydrate 89g (Dietary Fiber 12g); Protein 25g.

Have a Minute?

Cook Italian sausage links and cut into slices; add in step 3.

COME AND EAT!

Serve this dish with a loaf of Italian bread.

Fettuccine with Ricotta, Tomato and Basil

3 SERVINGS

Ricotta is a white, moist, subtly sweet cheese with a slightly grainy texture. It is a popular ingredient in many Italian dishes.

Have a Minute?

Add diced prosciutto or ham in step 3.

COME AND EAT!

Toss fresh basil leaves together with mixed greens and sprinkle with crumbled blue cheese or Gorgonzola for a splendid salad.

1 package (9 ounces) refrigerated uncooked fettuccine

3 tablespoons margarine or butter, melted

3/4 cup ricotta cheese

1/2 cup grated Parmesan cheese

1 large tomato, chopped (1 cup)

2 tablespoons coarsely chopped fresh basil leaves

1. Cook and drain fettuccine as directed on package. Return to saucepan.

2. Mix margarine, ricotta cheese and 1/3 cup of the Parmesan cheese; toss with fettuccine.

3. Serve fettuccine topped with tomato, basil and remaining Parmesan cheese.

1 Serving: Calories 550 (Calories from Fat 215); Fat 24g (Saturated 9g); Cholesterol 105mg; Sodium 480mg; Carbohydrate 62g (Dietary Fiber 3g); Protein 24g.

Fettuccine with Ricotta, Tomato and Basil

Caesar Tortellini

4 SERVINGS

The varieties of tortellini available in the refrigerated section of the grocery store are growing. Try some of the other flavors as well in this recipe.

Have a Minute?

Add grilled chicken or beef, cut into strips for a heartier meal.

COME AND EAT!

Surprise everyone by serving apple or cherry crisp for dessert—no one will know you didn't even bake it! Heat canned apple or cherry pie filling and top with granola and whipped cream.

---

1 package (9 ounces) refrigerated uncooked cheese-filled tortellini

1 package (7 1/2 ounces) complete Caesar salad mix

1 medium tomato, chopped (3/4 cup)

1/4 cup imitation bacon-flavor bits

1/4 teaspoon freshly ground pepper

1. Cook and drain tortellini as directed on package. Rinse with cold water; drain.

2. Toss tortellini, all ingredients in salad mix and remaining ingredients. Serve immediately.

1 Serving: Calories 230 (Calories from Fat 55); Fat 6g (Saturated 3g); Cholesterol 25mg; Sodium 310mg; Carbohydrate 33g (Dietary Fiber 2g); Protein 13g.

Caesar Tortellini

Chili Beef 'n' Noodles

4 SERVINGS

This recipe is guaranteed to become a family favorite you'll make again and again.

Have a Minute?

Company coming? Add a bit of pizzazz by stirring in 1/4 cup each whole pimiento-stuffed green and pitted ripe olives with soup and salsa in step 2.

COME AND EAT!

Top slices of purchased pound cake with warm peach slices (fresh, frozen or canned peach pie filling) drizzled with caramel ice cream topping. Add a dollop of whipped cream and you'll have a true crowd pleaser.

4 cups uncooked wide egg noodles (8 ounces)

1 pound ground beef

1 medium onion, chopped (1/2 cup)

1 can (11 1/4 ounces) condensed fiesta chili beef with beans soup

1 jar (8 ounces) salsa (1 cup)

1/2 cup water

1 cup shredded Cheddar cheese (4 ounces)

1. Cook and drain noodles as directed on package.

2. While noodles are cooking, cook beef and onion in 12-inch skillet over medium-high heat, stirring occasionally, until beef is brown; drain. Reduce heat to medium. Stir in soup, salsa and water. Cook until thoroughly heated.

3. Serve beef mixture over noodles. Sprinkle with cheese.

1 Serving: Calories 650 (Calories from Fat 280); Fat 31g (Saturated 14g); Cholesterol 155mg; Sodium 950mg; Carbohydrate 57g (Dietary Fiber 5g); Protein 41g.

Spiced Chicken and Apricot Couscous

6 SERVINGS

Use your kitchen scissors to quickly cut up the apricots for this recipe.

2 tablespoons olive or vegetable oil

1 pound skinless, boneless chicken breast halves, cut into 1-inch pieces

1 cup dried apricots, cut up

1 1/4 teaspoons ground cinnamon

1/4 teaspoon ground allspice

1 can (14 1/2 ounces) chicken broth

3/4 cup uncooked couscous

1 cup sliced almonds

3 tablespoons chopped fresh basil leaves

1. Heat oil in 12-inch skillet over medium-high heat. Cook chicken in oil, stirring frequently, until brown.

2. Stir in apricots, cinnamon, allspice and broth; heat to boiling.

3. Stir in couscous; remove from heat. Cover and let stand about 5 minutes or until liquid is absorbed. Add almonds and basil; toss gently.

1 Serving: Calories 360 (Calories from Fat 145); Fat 16g (Saturated 3g); Cholesterol 40mg; Sodium 340mg; Carbohydrate 35g (Dietary Fiber 5g); Protein 24g.

Have a Minute?

Add 1/2 cup sliced green onions in step 2.

COME AND EAT!

Serve with a salad of sliced cucumber, chopped tomato and a dressing of plain yogurt spiked with crushed red pepper and chopped fresh mint.

Wild Mushroom Pizzas

4 SERVINGS

Cut into wedges, these pizzas are also a great idea if you need an appetizer, fast.

—*Have a Minute?*—

Sliced bell pepper strips would add a colorful accent to this earthy pizza.

COME AND EAT!

Want a zesty Italian salad? Combine purchased salad mix containing iceberg lettuce, shredded carrot and red cabbage. Add pepperoni slices, sliced olives, red onion rings, whole pepperocini, cherry tomatoes, croutons, Parmesan cheese and toss with Italian dressing.

4 flour tortillas (8 to 10 inches in diameter)

1/4 cup margarine or butter

1 pound wild mushrooms (crimini, oyster, shiitake), sliced

2 medium onions, thinly sliced

1/4 cup cider vinegar

1 teaspoon dried thyme leaves

3 cups shredded mozzarella cheese (12 ounces)

1/2 cup grated Parmesan cheese

1. Heat oven to 400°. Place tortillas on ungreased cookie sheet. Bake 5 to 10 minutes or until crisp.

2. While tortillas are baking, melt margarine in 12-inch nonstick skillet over medium-high heat. Cook mushrooms and onions in margarine, stirring occasionally, until tender. Stir in vinegar and thyme. Cook 1 minute, stirring occasionally.

3. Spread mushroom mixture on tortillas; sprinkle with cheeses. Bake 5 to 8 minutes or until cheese is melted.

1 Serving: Calories 565 (Calories from Fat 290); Fat 32g (Saturated 15g); Cholesterol 55mg; Sodium 980mg; Carbohydrate 38g (Dietary Fiber 3g); Protein 34g.

Pizza Quesadillas

4 SERVINGS

Pepperoni pizza lovers will be hooked on this pizza option.

8 flour tortillas (8 to 10 inches in diameter)

4 cups shredded mozzarella cheese (16 ounces)

1 package (3 ounces) sliced pepperoni

1/2 can (14 1/2-ounce size) chunky tomatoes with olive oil, garlic and spices, undrained and, if desired, warmed

1. Heat 12-inch nonstick skillet over medium heat. Place 1 tortilla in skillet. Sprinkle with 1/2 cup of the cheese. Top with 1/4 of the pepperoni. Sprinkle with additional 1/2 cup cheese. Top with another tortilla.

2. Cook 2 to 3 minutes or until bottom is golden brown; turn. Cook 2 to 3 minutes longer or until bottom is golden brown.

3. Repeat 3 more times with remaining tortillas, cheese and pepperoni. Cut each quesadilla into wedges. Serve with tomatoes.

TIP: To keep quesadillas warm, place on ungreased cookie sheet in 250° oven.

1 Serving: Calories 695 (Calories from Fat 315); Fat 35g (Saturated 17g); Cholesterol 80mg; Sodium 1580mg; Carbohydrate 55g (Dietary Fiber 3g); Protein 43g.

Have a Minute?

Drain a 2.5-ounce can of sliced mushrooms and arrange over pepperoni in step 1.

COME AND EAT!

Quadruple chocolate malts are so easy to make! Combine 1/2 cup chocolate milk, 1/4 cup chocolate fudge ice cream topping, 1/4 cup chocolate malted milk powder and 1 quart (4 cups) chocolate ice cream in a blender. Cover and blend until smooth.

Chicken Enchilada Pizzas

4 SERVINGS

Have a Minute?

Chop 1 large tomato and sprinkle on after chicken mixture, but before cheese in step 3.

COME AND EAT!

Thaw and drain a 16-ounce bag of your favorite frozen vegetable combination and toss with your favorite salad dressing for a super easy salad.

4 flour tortillas (8 to 10 inches in diameter)

1 tablespoon vegetable oil

1 medium onion, thinly sliced

2 cups chopped cooked chicken breast

1/2 cup green salsa

1 can (2 1/4 ounces) sliced ripe olives, drained

1/3 cup sour cream

2 cups shredded Monterey Jack cheese (8 ounces)

1. Heat oven to 400°. Place tortillas on ungreased cookie sheet. Bake 5 to 10 minutes or until crisp.

2. While tortillas are baking, heat oil in 10-inch nonstick skillet over medium heat. Cook onion in oil, stirring frequently, until tender; remove from heat. Stir in chicken, salsa and olives.

3. Spread sour cream on tortillas. Top with chicken mixture and cheese. Bake 5 to 8 minutes or until cheese is melted.

1 Serving: Calories 540 (Calories from Fat 280); Fat 31g (Saturated 15g); Cholesterol 120mg; Sodium 810mg; Carbohydrate 30g (Dietary Fiber 3g); Protein 38g.

Italian Vegetable Pizza

6 SERVINGS

There's no need to order out when you can make pizza at home so easily.

1 package (16 ounces) Italian bread shell or ready-to-serve pizza crust (12 to 14 inches in diameter)

1/3 cup pesto

1/2 package (16-ounce size) frozen stir-fry bell peppers and onions (2 1/2 cups)

1 jar (4 1/2 ounces) sliced mushrooms, drained

2 cups shredded Italian blend cheese (8 ounces)

1/2 cup marinated sun-dried tomatoes, cut up

1. Heat oven to 400°. Place bread shell on ungreased cookie sheet. Spread with pesto.

2. Rinse frozen bell pepper mixture with cold water to separate; drain. Spread pepper mixture and mushrooms over pesto. Sprinkle with cheese and tomatoes.

3. Bake 8 to 12 minutes or until cheese is melted.

1 Serving: Calories 345 (Calories from Fat 170); Fat 19g (Saturated 7g); Cholesterol 26mg; Sodium 570mg; Carbohydrate 26g (Dietary Fiber 1g); Protein 18g.

Have a Minute?

Top pesto with strips of grilled chicken or cut-up frozen cooked meatballs (thawed) for a meatier twist.

COME AND EAT!

Impressive desserts can be deceptively simple. Split an 8- or 9-inch purchased angel food cake horizontally into 4 layers. Place bottom layer on a serving plate and spread with 1/3 can of raspberry or strawberry pie filling. Repeat with the next 2 layers and then put on top layer. Frost the top and sides with an 8-ounce container of frozen whipped topping (thawed). Sprinkle with grated chocolate.

Shrimp and Feta Pizza

6 SERVINGS

Here's a pizza for those who enjoy exploring new flavor combinations.

Have a Minute?

Sprinkle pizza with 1/4 to 1/3 cup pine nuts on top of cheeses in step 3.

COME AND EAT!

Serve with fresh cut-up fruit drizzled with your favorite fruit-flavored yogurt that has been combined with a little honey.

1 package (16 ounces) Italian bread shell or ready-to-serve pizza crust (12 to 14 inches in diameter)

1 tablespoon olive or vegetable oil

1/2 pound uncooked peeled deveined medium shrimp, thawed if frozen

1 clove garlic, finely chopped

2 cups shredded mozzarella cheese (8 ounces)

1 can (2 1/4 ounces) sliced ripe olives, drained

1 cup crumbled feta cheese

1 tablespoon chopped fresh or 1 teaspoon dried rosemary leaves

1. Heat oven to 400°. Place bread shell on ungreased cookie sheet.

2. Heat oil in 10-inch nonstick skillet over medium heat. Cook shrimp and garlic in oil about 3 minutes, stirring frequently, until shrimp are pink and firm.

3. Sprinkle bread shell with 1 cup of the mozzarella cheese. Top with shrimp, olives, remaining 1 cup mozzarella cheese and the feta cheese. Sprinkle with rosemary. Bake about 15 minutes or until cheese is melted.

1 Serving: Calories 350 (Calories from Fat 160); Fat 18g (Saturated 9g); Cholesterol 100mg; Sodium 840mg; Carbohydrate 22g (Dietary Fiber 0g); Protein 25g.

Shrimp and Feta Pizza

Indian Curried Turkey Pizzas

4 SERVINGS

Pita bread makes an excellent crust for single-serve pizzas. Experiment with a variety of toppings, such as those suggested in this recipe.

Have a Minute?

Sprinkle pizza with 1/4 to 1/3 cup chopped peanuts or cashews with the bacon bits in step 2.

COME AND EAT!

Cook desired amount instant white rice; stir in prepared vanilla pudding (warm or cold) and raisins and sprinkle with cinnamon for creamy, no-bake rice pudding.

4 pita bread folds or regular pita breads (6 inches in diameter)

1/2 cup mayonnaise or salad dressing

1 teaspoon curry powder

2/3 cup frozen green peas

3 cups shredded mozzarella cheese (12 ounces)

1/4 pound deli sliced cooked turkey breast, cut into strips

1 large tomato, chopped (1 cup)

1/4 cup imitation bacon-flavor bits

1. Heat oven to 400°. Place pita breads on ungreased cookie sheet. Mix mayonnaise and curry powder. Spread evenly over pitas.

2. Rinse peas with cold water to separate; drain. Sprinkle 1/4 cup of the cheese over each pita. Top with peas, turkey, tomato and bacon bits. Top with remaining cheese.

3. Bake 10 to 12 minutes or until cheese is melted.

1 Serving: Calories 675 (Calories from Fat 360); Fat 40g (Saturated 14g); Cholesterol 75mg; Sodium 1430mg; Carbohydrate 45g (Dietary Fiber 4g); Protein 38g.

Indian Curried Turkey Pizzas

5

Sensational Soups, Salads and Sandwiches

Southwest Cheese Soup (page 106)

Southwest Cheese Soup

4 SERVINGS

Cheese soup does not have to be difficult or time consuming to prepare. Here's an unbelievably easy cheese soup.

Have a Minute?

Stir in 1/2 pound browned ground beef or chorizo sausage in step 1 for a warming, substantial meal.

COME AND EAT!

Serve with corn muffins and for dessert, cool off with frozen margarita pie. Mix together 1 quart (4 cups) softened vanilla ice cream, one 6-ounce can of frozen limeade (thawed), 2 tablespoons orange juice and 2 tablespoons of tequila, if desired. Spoon into a purchased 9-inch chocolate or graham cracker crust. Freeze about 4 hours or until firm.

1 cup milk

1 package (16 ounces) process cheese spread loaf, cut into cubes

1 can (15 1/4 ounces) whole kernel corn, drained

1 can (15 ounces) black beans, rinsed and drained

1 can (10 ounces) diced tomatoes and green chilies, undrained

Chopped fresh cilantro, if desired

1. Mix all ingredients except cilantro in 3-quart saucepan.

2. Cook over medium-low heat, stirring frequently, until cheese is melted and soup is hot. Sprinkle each serving with cilantro.

1 Serving: Calories 620 (Calories from Fat 260); Fat 29g (Saturated 17g); Cholesterol 70mg; Sodium 2660mg; Carbohydrate 65g (Dietary Fiber 10g); Protein 35g.

Creamy Wild Rice and Vegetable Chowder

6 SERVINGS

This recipe eliminates the time-consuming step of precooking wild rice.

2 tablespoons margarine or butter

1 large onion, chopped (1 cup)

2 medium carrots, thinly sliced (1 cup)

1 package (8 ounces) sliced mushrooms (3 cups)

2 cups chicken broth

1 package (6.2 ounces) fast-cooking long grain and wild rice

1 can (15 1/4 ounces) whole kernel corn, drained

1 can (10 3/4 ounces) condensed cream of potato soup

2 cups milk

1. Melt margarine in 3-quart saucepan over medium-high heat. Cook onion, carrots and mushrooms in margarine, stirring occasionally, until tender.

2. Stir in broth, rice and contents of seasoning packet from rice. Heat to boiling; reduce heat to low. Cover and simmer about 5 minutes or until liquid is absorbed.

3. Stir in corn, soup and milk; cook until hot.

1 Serving: Calories 250 (Calories from Fat 90); Fat 10g (Saturated 3g); Cholesterol 10mg; Sodium 860mg; Carbohydrate 34g (Dietary Fiber 3g); Protein 9g.

Have a Minute?

Soup is perfect for casual get-togethers. Make it "souper-douper" by adding 1 cup diced ham and 1/2 cup toasted sliced almonds in step 3.

COME AND EAT!

Brush purchased soft breadsticks with Italian salad dressing and sprinkle with grated Parmesan cheese. Bake until golden brown.

Italian Tomato-Bread Soup

4 SERVINGS

Have a Minute?

To turn this into a pizza soup, stir in 1 pound of browned Italian sausage and one 2 1/2-ounce can of sliced mushrooms (drained) in step 1.

COME AND EAT!

Serve with a simple tossed salad with creamy Italian dressing.

1 cup water
2 cans (14 1/2 ounces each) chunky tomatoes with olive oil, garlic and spices, undrained
1 can (11 1/2 ounces) tomato juice
4 slices rosemary, Italian or French bread, 1/2 inch thick
2 tablespoons pesto
2 tablespoons shredded Parmesan cheese

1. Heat water, tomatoes and juice to boiling in 3-quart saucepan.

2. Set oven control to broil. Place bread on cookie sheet. Spread with pesto; sprinkle with cheese. Broil with tops 4 to 6 inches from heat 1 to 2 minutes or until edges of bread are golden brown.

3. Ladle soup into 4 soup bowls. Top each serving with bread slice.

1 Serving: Calories 190 (Calories from Fat 65); Fat 7g (Saturated 2g); Cholesterol 5mg; Sodium 1070mg; Carbohydrate 29g (Dietary Fiber 3g); Protein 6g.

Ham and Green Bean Soup

6 SERVINGS

Have a Minute?

Place about 2 tablespoons of shredded Cheddar or mozzarella cheese into the bottom of each soup bowl before adding soup.

COME AND EAT!

Serve thick slices of bread with soup. For those who don't like to dip their bread into the soup, serve margarine or butter.

2 cups cubed fully cooked ham
3/4 teaspoon dried thyme leaves
1/4 teaspoon pepper
1 package (16 ounces) frozen green beans, potatoes, onions and red peppers
2 cans (14 1/2 ounces each) chicken broth
Sour cream, if desired

1. Mix all ingredients except sour cream in 2-quart saucepan. Heat to boiling; reduce heat to medium-low. Simmer uncovered 6 to 8 minutes, stirring occasionally, until vegetables are tender.

2. Top each serving with sour cream.

1 Serving: Calories 135 (Calories from Fat 45); Fat 5g (Saturated 2g); Cholesterol 25mg; Sodium 1300mg; Carbohydrate 10g (Dietary Fiber 2g); Protein 14g.

Italian Tomato-Bread Soup

Bagels with Roast Beef, Cream Cheese and Mustard-Caper Sauce

4 SERVINGS

On your next shopping trip, pick up the ingredients for these sandwiches to have on hand for one of your dinners this week.

Have a Minute?

Try out those new dill pickles referred to as sandwich slices and place on bagels after spreading with the cream cheese mixture in step 1.

COME AND EAT!

Potato salad or potato chips, and cut-up assorted raw vegetables will complete this tasty meal.

2 tablespoons honey mustard

1 tablespoon Dijon mustard

1 tablespoon finely chopped red onion

1 tablespoon capers, drained and chopped

1/2 teaspoon dried dill weed

4 soft bagels, split

1/2 cup soft cream cheese

1/2 pound thinly sliced cooked roast beef

4 lettuce leaves

1. Mix mustards, onion, capers and dill weed.

2. Spread each bagel half with cream cheese. Spread 4 bagel halves with mustard mixture. Top with roast beef, lettuce leaf and remaining bagel halves.

1 Serving: Calories 360 (Calories from Fat 125); Fat 14g (Saturated 8g); Cholesterol 80mg; Sodium 630mg; Carbohydrate 33g (Dietary Fiber 2g); Protein 27g.

Bagels with Roast Beef, Cream Cheese and Mustard-Caper Sauce

Burrito BLT Sandwiches

6 SERVINGS

Have a Minute?

Spread each tortilla with 2 tablespoons guacamole before adding bacon mixture. Ole!

Come and Eat!

Cinnamon fried ice cream without frying? Coarsely crush Cinnamon Toast Crunch® cereal over scoops of vanilla or chocolate ice cream—easy!

8 slices bacon, crisply cooked and crumbled

2 cups bite-size pieces lettuce

1 1/2 cups shredded Cheddar cheese (6 ounces)

1 large tomato, chopped (1 cup)

1/3 cup mayonnaise or salad dressing

6 flour tortillas (8 to 10 inches in diameter)

1. Toss all ingredients, except tortillas.

2. Place one-sixth of bacon mixture on each tortilla. Fold up bottom third of each tortilla; roll up to form cone shape with folded end at bottom.

1 Serving: Calories 360 (Calories from Fat 207); Fat 23g (Saturated 9g); Cholesterol 40mg; Sodium 590mg; Carbohydrate 27g (Dietary Fiber 2g); Protein 14g.

Thai Turkey Burrito Sandwiches

4 SERVINGS

Have a Minute?

Stir 1 cup of cold cooked rice along with the cole-slaw mixture in step 1.

Come and Eat!

Drain one 29-ounce can of pear halves and place in 9-inch pie plate. Drizzle with caramel ice cream topping. Bake at 350° for 8 to 12 minutes until warm. Sprinkle with cinnamon and toasted pecans if you'd like.

1/4 cup vegetable oil

2 tablespoons seasoned rice vinegar

2 tablespoons peanut butter

1 tablespoon soy sauce

Dash of ground red pepper (cayenne)

3 cups coleslaw mix

4 flour tortillas (8 to 10 inches in diameter)

8 slices deli sliced cooked turkey breast (1/2 pound)

1. Mix oil, vinegar, peanut butter, soy sauce and red pepper in medium bowl. Toss with coleslaw mix.

2. Top each tortilla with 2 slices turkey. Place one-fourth of coleslaw mixture on one end of each tortilla; roll up.

1 Serving: Calories 405 (Calories from Fat 207); Fat 23g (Saturated 4g); Cholesterol 40mg; Sodium 550mg; Carbohydrate 29g (Dietary Fiber 3g); Protein 24g.

Burrito BLT Sandwiches

Chicken Caesar Sandwiches

4 SERVINGS

Here's a classic Italian salad in sandwich form. Purchased washed and torn salad greens of romaine or a romaine blend makes preparation of this sandwich much easier.

Have a Minute?

To add a sophisticated touch, place roasted red pepper pieces (from a jar) on the focaccia after spreading with the dressing.

COME AND EAT!

Serve cooked Italian green beans, broccoli or asparagus.

4 skinless, boneless chicken breast halves (about 1 pound)

3 cups romaine pieces (from 10-ounce package)

2 tablespoons grated Parmesan cheese

1/2 cup creamy Caesar dressing

1 round loaf cheese-and-herb focaccia bread (12 inches in diameter)

1. Spray 12-inch skillet with nonstick cooking spray and heat over medium-high heat. Cook chicken in skillet 12 to 15 minutes, turning once, until juice is no longer pink when centers of thickest pieces are cut.

2. While chicken is cooking, toss romaine, cheese and 1/4 cup of the dressing.

3. Cut focaccia horizontally in half; cut into fourths. Spread cut sides of bread with remaining 1/4 cup of the dressing. Top each bottom fourth of focaccia with chicken breast half, one-fourth of the romaine mixture and tops of focaccia.

1 Serving: Calories 650 (Calories from Fat 225); Fat 25g (Saturated 6g); Cholesterol 70mg; Sodium 1810mg; Carbohydrate 73g (Dietary Fiber 3g); Protein 36g.

Warm Chicken-Potato Salad

4 SERVINGS

This salad can be made ahead and served cold.

8 small red potatoes, cut into 1/2-inch cubes
1 1/2 cups frozen cut green beans
1 1/2 cups cubed cooked chicken breast
3/4 cup refrigerated dill dip

1. Heat 1 inch water (salted, if desired) to boiling in 2-quart saucepan. Add potatoes. Cook over medium-high heat about 10 minutes or until tender.

2. Place green beans in colander. Drain potatoes and thaw green beans by pouring the potatoes with the cooking liquid over green beans.

3. Toss potatoes, green beans, chicken and dill dip.

1 Serving: Calories 355 (Calories from Fat 80); Fat 9g (Saturated 5g); Cholesterol 55mg; Sodium 370mg; Carbohydrate 52g (Dietary Fiber 6g); Protein 22g.

Have a Minute?

Chop up one small red, yellow or orange bell pepper and add in step 3.

COME AND EAT!

Split hot dog or hamburger buns and spread with ranch salad dressing; sprinkle with green onions and grated Parmesan cheese. Broil about 1 minute until topping starts to bubble.

Greek Bread Salad

6 SERVINGS

"Refreshing and flavorful" describes this tossed salad.

Have a Minute?

Lemons are a staple ingredient in Greek cuisine. Grate 1 teaspoon lemon peel and toss with ingredients in step 1.

COME AND EAT!

Baklava is a traditional Greek dessert made from phyllo dough, honey syrup, spices and nuts. This shortcut version has the same flavors but is made in a fraction of the time. Place one refrigerated pie crust on a cookie sheet and cut into 12 wedges; bake according to package directions. Brush 6 wedges with honey; sprinkle with cinnamon, nutmeg and cloves. Sprinkle with chopped nuts. Place another wedge on top of the nuts; repeat to form 6 dessert wedges.

1/2 package (10-ounce size) romaine pieces (4 cups)

1/2 pound deli sliced cooked roast beef, cut into thin strips

2 large tomatoes, cut into 1-inch pieces

1/2 yellow bell pepper, cut into 1-inch pieces

1 can (2 1/4 ounces) sliced ripe olives, drained

2/3 cup crumbled feta cheese (about 3 ounces)

2/3 cup Italian dressing

4 slices French or Italian bread (1/2 inch thick), cut into cubes

1. Gently toss all ingredients except bread cubes in large bowl.

2. Set oven control to broil. Place bread cubes on cookie sheet. Broil with tops 4 to 6 inches from heat about 2 minutes, stirring once, until crisp and golden brown.

3. Add bread cubes to romaine mixture; toss. Serve immediately.

1 Serving: Calories 300 (Calories from Fat 198); Fat 22g (Saturated 6g); Cholesterol 50mg; Sodium 560mg; Carbohydrate 12g (Dietary Fiber 2g); Protein 14g.

Warm Cajun Rice Salad

6 SERVINGS

Cajun is hot, hot, hot! Adjust the red pepper sauce according to your heat tolerance.

1 1/2 cups uncooked instant rice

1 cup cubed fully cooked ham

1 large tomato, chopped (1 cup)

1 small green bell pepper, chopped (1/2 cup)

1 can (15 to 16 ounces) kidney beans, rinsed and drained

3 tablespoons olive or vegetable oil

3 tablespoons white vinegar

2 teaspoons Cajun or Creole seasoning

1 teaspoon red pepper sauce

1. Cook rice as directed on package.

2. Mix rice, ham, tomato, bell pepper and beans in large bowl.

3. Mix remaining ingredients; toss with rice mixture.

1 Serving: Calories 270 (Calories from Fat 90); Fat 10g (Saturated 2g); Cholesterol 15mg; Sodium 600mg; Carbohydrate 37g (Dietary Fiber 4g); Protein 12g.

Have a Minute?

Cut enough pickled okra pods to equal 1/3 cup and add in step 3.

COME AND EAT!

Layer cut-up pound cake or angel food cake with ready-to-eat vanilla pudding and raspberry or strawberry jam and nondairy whipped topping (thawed) in parfait glasses for instant trifle.

Tuscan Tuna Salad

4 SERVINGS

Beans are a common ingredient in recipes from the Tuscany region of Italy.

1/2 package (10-ounce size) Italian blend lettuce pieces (4 cups)

1 large tomato, coarsely chopped (1 cup)

1 can (15 to 16 ounces) great northern beans, rinsed and drained

1 can (9 ounces) tuna, drained

3 tablespoons chopped red onion

2 tablespoons olive or vegetable oil

1 tablespoon balsamic vinegar

1 tablespoon Dijon mustard

1/2 teaspoon dried dill weed

1. Gently toss lettuce, tomato, beans and tuna in large bowl.

2. Mix remaining ingredients; toss with tuna mixture just until coated. Serve immediately.

1 Serving: Calories 280 (Calories from Fat 72); Fat 8g (Saturated 1g); Cholesterol 20mg; Sodium 540mg; Carbohydrate 32g (Dietary Fiber 8g); Protein 28g.

Have a Minute?

Turn this into a Niçoise-style salad by adding sliced cooked potatoes in step 2.

COME AND EAT!

Broil French bread slices until one side is lightly toasted. Spread slices with olive-flavored cream cheese and sprinkle with mozzarella or shredded Parmesan cheese. Broil until cheese begins to melt. Olive crostini in a flash!

Tuscan Tuna Salad

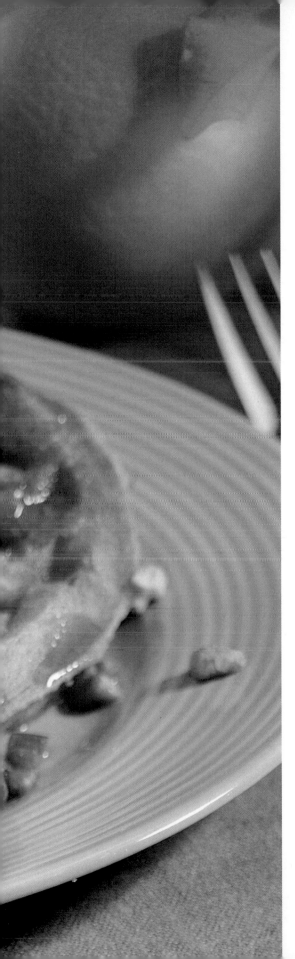

6

Breakfast for Dinner

Pumpkin Waffles with Maple-Apple Syrup (page 134)

Breakfast Tacos

6 SERVINGS

As colorful as a Mexican serape or blanket, this dish is sure to become a weekend favorite.

Have a Minute?

Cook 6 brown-and-serve pork sausage links and cut into pieces; place pieces on top of eggs in step 3.

COME AND EAT!

Cook up some frozen or refrigerated hash browns to serve on the side.

4 eggs

1/4 teaspoon garlic salt

1/4 teaspoon pepper

1/4 cup chopped green bell pepper

4 medium green onions, chopped (1/4 cup)

1 tablespoon margarine or butter

1/2 cup shredded Monterey Jack cheese with jalapeño peppers (2 ounces)

6 taco shells

1 cup shredded lettuce

1 small avocado, sliced (3/4 cup)

1/4 cup thick-and-chunky salsa

1. Beat eggs, garlic salt and pepper thoroughly with fork. Stir in bell pepper and onions.

2. Melt margarine in 8-inch skillet over medium heat. Pour egg mixture into skillet. As mixture begins to set at bottom and side, gently lift cooked portions with spatula so that thin, uncooked portions can flow to bottom. Avoid constant stirring. Cook 3 to 4 minutes or until eggs are thickened throughout but still moist. Gently stir in cheese.

3. Heat taco shells as directed on package. Place lettuce in taco shells. Spoon eggs onto lettuce. Top with avocado and salsa.

1 Serving: Calories 205 (Calories from Fat 135); Fat 15g (Saturated 5g); Cholesterol 150mg; Sodium 240mg; Carbohydrate 12g (Dietary Fiber 3g); Protein 8g.

Sausage and Egg Breakfast Pizza

4 SERVINGS

Kids of all ages will love the idea of eating pizza for breakfast!

Have a Minute?

For variety, add additional ingredients such as chopped tomato, green bell pepper or mushrooms before topping with the final cheese layer.

COME AND EAT!

Fresh grapefruit halves or sections, sold in jars in the produce department, would give this breakfast spunk.

1 package (8 ounces) frozen brown-and-serve pork sausage links, cut into 1/2-inch pieces

6 eggs, beaten

2 packages (8 ounces each) Italian bread shells or 4 pita breads (6 inches in diameter)

1 1/2 cups shredded Cheddar cheese (6 ounces)

1. Heat oven to 400°. Spray 10-inch nonstick skillet with cooking spray; heat over medium heat. Cook sausage in skillet about 3 minutes, stirring occasionally, until brown. Remove sausage from skillet; set aside.

2. Pour eggs into same skillet. As eggs begin to set at bottom and side, gently lift cooked portions with spatula so that thin, uncooked portion can flow to bottom. Avoid constant stirring. Cook 3 to 4 minutes or until eggs are thickened throughout but still moist.

3. Place bread shells on ungreased cookie sheet. Sprinkle with half of the cheese. Top with eggs and sausage. Sprinkle with remaining cheese. Bake 10 to 12 minutes or until cheese is melted.

1 Serving: Calories 640 (Calories from Fat 380); Fat 42g (Saturated 19g); Cholesterol 420mg; Sodium 1390mg; Carbohydrate 27g (Dietary Fiber 0g); Protein 38g.

Home-Style Scrambled Eggs

4 SERVINGS

Do your scrambled eggs end up looking more like rice or peas than the fluffy, moist, thick eggs from a restaurant? The trick is to avoid stirring them as much as possible while they cook.

6 eggs

3/4 teaspoon salt

3 tablespoons water

1/4 cup margarine or butter

1 cup refrigerated diced potatoes with onions or frozen hash brown potatoes

1 small zucchini, chopped (1 cup)

1 medium tomato, seeded and chopped (3/4 cup)

1. Beat eggs, salt and water.

2. Melt margarine in 10-inch skillet over medium heat. Cook potatoes, zucchini and tomato in margarine, stirring occasionally, until hot.

3. Pour egg mixture over vegetable mixture. As mixture begins to set at bottom and side, gently lift cooked portions with spatula so that thin, uncooked portion can flow to bottom. Avoid constant stirring. Cook 3 to 4 minutes or until eggs are thickened throughout but still moist.

1 Serving: Calories 250 (Calories from Fat 170); Fat 19g (Saturated 5g); Cholesterol 320mg; Sodium 780mg; Carbohydrate 10g (Dietary Fiber 1g); Protein 11g.

Have a Minute?

Perk up these eggs with a liberal dose of shredded sharp Cheddar or Colby cheese added during the last few minutes of cooking.

COME AND EAT!

Can you smell the bacon cooking? It's the perfect addition to this hearty country-style meal.

Smoked Sausage and Eggs

6 SERVINGS

Here's a recipe for comfort food without the work.

Have a Minute?

Cut up 2 medium apples and cook with potatoes and sausage in step 1. Leave the peel on for extra color.

COME AND EAT!

Remember cinnamon-sugar toast? Enjoy it again! Toast slices of white bread; butter and sprinkle with sugar and cinnamon.

2 tablespoons vegetable oil

1 package (24 ounces) frozen diced potatoes with onions and peppers

1 package (16 ounces) smoked beef sausage ring, cut into 1/2-inch slices

3/4 teaspoon dried basil leaves

3/4 teaspoon dried thyme leaves

6 eggs

1. Heat oil in 12-inch nonstick skillet over medium-high heat. Cook potatoes, sausage, basil and thyme in oil 10 minutes, stirring frequently.

2. Make 6 indentations in potato mixture with back of spoon. Break 1 egg into each indentation. Reduce heat to medium-low. Cover and cook 3 to 4 minutes or until egg whites and yolks are firm, not runny.

1 Serving: Calories 435 (Calories from Fat 280); Fat 31g (Saturated 12g); Cholesterol 260mg; Sodium 1370mg; Carbohydrate 22g (Dietary Fiber 2g); Protein 17g.

Eggs with Kielbasa

4 SERVINGS

Kielbasa is a smoked Polish sausage made usually from pork, although beef can be added. It comes in a horseshoe-shaped ring, about 1 1/2 inches in diameter.

2 teaspoons vegetable oil

1/2 pound kielbasa, cut lengthwise in half then crosswise into slices

1 large onion, sliced

1 medium green bell pepper, thinly sliced

8 eggs

1/2 cup milk

1/4 teaspoon salt

1/8 to 1/4 teaspoon pepper

1. Heat oil in 10-inch skillet over medium heat. Cook kielbasa, onion and bell pepper in oil about 5 minutes, stirring occasionally, until vegetables are tender.

2. While kielbasa mixture is cooking, beat eggs, milk, salt and pepper.

3. Pour egg mixture over kielbasa mixture. As mixture begins to set at bottom and side, gently lift cooked portions with spatula so that thin, uncooked portion can flow to bottom. Avoid constant stirring. Cook 4 to 5 minutes or until eggs are thickened throughout but still moist.

1 Serving: Calories 375 (Calories from Fat 260); Fat 29g (Saturated 10g); Cholesterol 460mg; Sodium 860mg; Carbohydrate 8g (Dietary Fiber 1g); Protein 21g.

Have a Minute?

Cook 2 cups of coleslaw mix with the sausage, onion and green bell pepper in step 1.

COME AND EAT!

A fruity breakfast shake instead of orange juice is a welcome break in the routine. In a blender container, add equal amounts of orange juice and fruit-flavored yogurt, and sweeten with a drizzle of honey. Blend until smooth.

Teriyaki Vegetable Medley with Eggs

4 SERVINGS

Only three ingredients! This recipe takes advantage of the frozen vegetable mixtures now available that come with a separate sauce packet.

Have a Minute?

Drain one 4-ounce can of tiny shrimp and add during the last few minutes of cooking the vegetables in step 1.

COME AND EAT!

Serve with fresh orange slices and toast.

1 package (1 pound 5 ounces) frozen broccoli, sugar snap peas, water chestnuts and red peppers with teriyaki sauce

2 tablespoons margarine or butter

8 eggs, beaten

1. Cook vegetables and sauce in 10-inch nonstick skillet over medium heat about 7 minutes, stirring frequently, until vegetables are crisp-tender. Remove mixture from skillet; keep warm.

2. Melt margarine in same skillet over medium heat. Pour eggs into skillet. As eggs begin to set at bottom and side, gently lift cooked portions with spatula so that thin, uncooked portion can flow to bottom. Avoid constant stirring. Cook 4 to 5 minutes or until eggs are thickened throughout but still moist.

3. Top eggs with vegetable mixture. Cut into wedges to serve.

1 Serving: Calories 320 (Calories from Fat 145); Fat 16g (Saturated 5g); Cholesterol 425mg; Sodium 440mg; Carbohydrate 19g (Dietary Fiber 3g); Protein 14g.

Teriyaki Vegetable Medley with Eggs

Ham and Apple Pancakes

ABOUT 15 PANCAKES

These hearty pancakes already have ham in them, so there is no need to cook up anything additional on the side.

Have a Minute?

If you're feeling just a tad adventurous, consider livening up the pancakes by adding 1 tablespoon Dijon mustard to the batter in step 1.

COME AND EAT!

Fresh grapes or melon slices are all that's needed to finish this meal.

1 can (21 ounces) apple pie filling
2 cups Bisquick Original baking mix
1 cup milk
2 eggs
3/4 cup diced fully cooked ham
1/2 cup shredded Cheddar cheese (2 ounces)
1 medium green onion, sliced (2 tablespoons), if desired
Cinnamon, if desired

1. Heat pie filling until hot; keep warm.

2. Heat griddle or skillet over medium heat or to 375°. Grease griddle with margarine if necessary. Beat baking mix, milk and eggs with wire whisk or hand beater in large bowl until smooth. Fold in ham, cheese and onion.

3. Pour batter by scant 1/4 cupfuls onto hot griddle. Cook until edges are dry. Turn; cook until golden brown. Serve with warm pie filling; sprinkle with cinnamon.

1 Pancake: Calories 150 (Calories from Fat 45); Fat 5g (Saturated 2g); Cholesterol 40mg; Sodium 380mg; Carbohydrate 22g (Dietary Fiber 1g); Protein 5g.

Pancake and Sausage Stacks

4 SERVINGS

Why not pancakes for dinner? Use your microwave to heat the pancakes.

┌─ *Have a Minute?* ─┐

Cheddar cheese, apples and sausage seem to have an affinity for each other. Sprinkle shredded Cheddar cheese between and on top of pancakes.

COME AND EAT!

Serve with fried refrigerated potato slices with chopped green onions.

1 package (7 ounces) frozen brown-and-serve pork sausage patties (8 patties)

2 medium apples, chopped (2 cups)

1 cup maple-flavored syrup

1/2 teaspoon ground cinnamon

8 packaged frozen pancakes

1. Mix all ingredients except pancakes in 12-inch nonstick skillet. Heat to boiling; reduce heat to medium. Cook about 5 minutes, stirring occasionally, until apples are tender.

2. Prepare pancakes as directed on package.

3. For each serving, place 2 sausage patties on 1 pancake; spoon apple mixture over sausage. Top with additional pancake and apple mixture.

1 Serving: Calories 580 (Calories from Fat 160); Fat 18g (Saturated 6g); Cholesterol 50mg; Sodium 1020mg; Carbohydrate 95g (Dietary Fiber 3g); Protein 13g.

Ham and Herbed Cheese Latkes

4 SERVINGS

Latkes, or potato pancakes, with their ethnic heritage are now becoming everyone's comfort food.

2 cups soft bread crumbs

1 cup chopped fully cooked ham

4 medium green onions, chopped (1/4 cup)

4 eggs, beaten

1/2 package (1-pound 4-ounce size) refrigerated shredded hash brown potatoes (1 1/2 cups)

1 container (5 ounces) herb- and garlic-flavored soft spreadable cheese

1 tablespoon vegetable oil

1/2 cup sour cream

1 medium green onion, chopped (1 tablespoon), if desired

1. Mix all ingredients except oil, sour cream and 1 green onion.

2. Heat oil in 12-inch nonstick skillet over medium heat. Spoon potato mixture into 4 mounds in skillet; flatten slightly. Cook 6 to 8 minutes, turning once, until deep golden brown.

3. Serve with sour cream; sprinkle with onion.

1 Serving: Calories 405 (Calories from Fat 270); Fat 30g (Saturated 15g); Cholesterol 295mg; Sodium 1020mg; Carbohydrate 13g (Dietary Fiber 1g); Protein 22g.

Have a Minute?

One 2-ounce jar of diced pimientos or 1 small red bell pepper, chopped, would add bright red color to these soft potato pancakes.

COME AND EAT!

Serve with fresh cut-up fruit and your favorite bakery muffins.

Pumpkin Waffles with Maple-Apple Syrup

6 (7 1/2-INCH) WAFFLES

No pumpkin pie spice on hand? Substitute 1/4 teaspoon each of ground cinnamon, ground nutmeg and ground ginger.

Have a Minute?

Grate 2 to 3 teaspoons orange peel for a vibrant citrus flavor and add in step 2. Garnish waffles with orange zest.

COME AND EAT!

Serve with cooked sausages, bacon or ham.

Maple-Apple Syrup (below)
2 1/3 cups Bisquick Original baking mix
1/2 cup canned pumpkin
1 1/2 cups milk
1/4 cup vegetable oil
2 tablespoons packed brown sugar
1 teaspoon pumpkin pie spice
2 eggs
1/4 cup chopped pecans

1. Prepare Maple-Apple Syrup; keep warm.

2. Heat waffle iron; grease if necessary. Beat remaining ingredients except pecans with wire whisk or hand beater until smooth.

3. Pour batter onto center of hot waffle iron. Bake until steaming stops and waffle is golden brown. Carefully remove waffle. Sprinkle with pecans. Serve with Maple-Apple Syrup.

MAPLE-APPLE SYRUP

1/2 cup maple-flavored syrup
1/4 cup frozen apple juice concentrate

Heat ingredients over medium heat, stirring occasionally, until juice concentrate is melted and mixture is warm.

One 7 1/2-inch Square: Calories 480 (Calories from Fat 200); Fat 22g (Saturated 5g); Cholesterol 75mg; Sodium 750mg; Carbohydrate 63g (Dietary Fiber 1g); Protein 8g.

Zucchini Pancakes

18 (3-INCH) PANCAKES

The shredded zucchini adds a great texture to these pancakes. It offers a great way to use up the summertime surplus.

2 eggs

1/3 cup Bisquick Original baking mix

1/4 cup grated Parmesan cheese

2 tablespoons chopped onion

Dash of pepper

1 medium zucchini, shredded (2 cups)

Ketchup or sour cream, if desired

1. Heat griddle or skillet over medium heat or to 375°. Grease griddle with margarine if necessary.

2. Beat eggs with hand beater in medium bowl until fluffy. Beat in remaining ingredients except zucchini until well blended. Fold in zucchini.

3. For each pancake, pour 2 tablespoons batter onto hot griddle; spread slightly with back of spoon. Cook until puffed and dry around edges. Turn; cook until golden brown. Serve with ketchup.

1 Pancake: Calories 20 (Calories from Fat 10); Fat 1g (Saturated 1g); Cholesterol 25mg; Sodium 60mg; Carbohydrate 2g (Dietary Fiber 0g); Protein 1g.

Have a Minute?

Shred one medium carrot into the batter to create pretty "vegetable confetti" pancakes.

COME AND EAT!

Cheese sauce, whether from a jar or homemade, would be great on these savory pancakes.

Fruited Gorgonzola and Cheddar Melts

4 OPEN-FACE SANDWICHES

COME AND EAT!

Frozen chocolate mousse is a simple, make-ahead dessert. Whip 2 cups whipping cream until stiff and fold in 1 1/4 cups almond, chocolate or coffee liqueur and 1/2 cup chocolate-flavored syrup. Pour into a square 9-inch pan and freeze for 4 hours. Serve with fresh raspberries.

4 slices bread, 1 inch thick

1 large apple, cored and cut into 8 rings

1 large pear, sliced

4 ounces Cheddar cheese, sliced

4 ounces Gorgonzola cheese, crumbled

1. Set oven control to broil. Place bread on ungreased cookie sheet. Broil with tops about 4 inches from heat 1 minute or until golden brown.

2. Turn bread. Divide apple rings and pear slices among bread slices. Top with cheeses. Broil 2 to 4 minutes or just until cheeses begin to melt.

1 Sandwich: Calories 345 (Calories from Fat 170); Fat 19g (Saturated 12g); Cholesterol 50mg; Sodium 710mg; Carbohydrate 31g (Dietary Fiber 3g); Protein 15g.

Fruited Gorgonzola and Cheddar Melts

Helpful Nutrition and Cooking Information

Nutrition Guidelines:

We provide nutrition information for each recipe that includes calories, fat, cholesterol, sodium, carbohydrate, fiber and protein. Individual food choices can be based on this information.

Recommended intake for a daily diet of 2,000 calories as set by the Food and Drug Administration:

Total Fat	Less than 65g
Saturated Fat	Less than 20g
Cholesterol	Less than 300mg
Sodium	Less than 2,400mg
Total Carbohydrate	300g
Dietary Fiber	25g

Criteria Used for Calculating Nutrition Information:

- The first ingredient is used wherever a choice is given (such as 1/3 cup sour cream or plain yogurt).

- The first ingredient amount is used wherever a range is given (such as 2 to 3 teaspoons milk).

- The first serving number is used wherever a range is given (such as 4 to 6 servings).

- "If desired" ingredients such as "two tablespoons brown sugar, if desired" and recipe variations are *not* included.

- Only the amount of a marinade or frying oil that is estimated to be absorbed by the food during preparation or cooking is calculated.

Cooking Terms Glossary:

Cooking has its own vocabulary just like many other creative activities. Here are some basic cooking terms to use as a handy reference.

Beat: Mix ingredients vigorously with spoon, fork, wire whisk, hand beater or electric mixer until smooth and uniform.

Blend: Mix ingredients with spoon, wire whisk or rubber scraper until very smooth and uniform. A blender, hand blender or food processor can be used.

Boil: Heat liquid until bubbles rise continuously and break on the surface and steam is given off. For rolling boil, the bubbles form rapidly.

Chop: Cut into coarse or fine irregular pieces with a knife, food chopper, blender or food processor.

Crisp-tender: Doneness description of vegetables cooked until tender but still retaining some of the crisp texture of the raw food.

Cube: Cut into squares 1/2 inch or larger.

Dice: Cut into squares smaller than 1/2 inch.

Grate: Cut into tiny particles using small rough holes of grater (citrus peel or chocolate).

Grease: Rub the inside surface of a pan with shortening, using pastry brush, piece of waxed paper or paper towel, to prevent food from sticking during baking (as for some casseroles).

Julienne: Cut into thin, matchlike strips, using knife or food processor (vegetables, fruits, meats).

Mix: Combine ingredients in any way that distributes them evenly.

Sauté: Cook foods in hot oil or margarine over medium-high heat with frequent tossing and turning motion.

Shred: Cut into long thin pieces by rubbing food across the holes of a shredder, as for cheese, or by using a knife to slice very thinly, as for cabbage.

Simmer: Cook in liquid just below the boiling point on top of the stove, usually after reducing heat from a boil. Bubbles will rise slowly and break just below the surface.

Stir: Mix ingredients until uniform consistency. Stir once in a while for stirring occasionally, often for stirring frequently and continuously for stirring constantly.

Toss: Tumble ingredients lightly with a lifting motion (such as green salad), usually to coat evenly or mix with another food.

Ingredients Used in Recipe Testing:

- White rice is used wherever cooked rice is listed in the ingredients, unless otherwise indicated.

- Ingredients used for testing represent those that the majority of consumers use in their homes: large eggs, canned ready-to-use chicken broth, and vegetable oil spread containing *not less than 65% fat.*

- Fat-free, low-fat or low-sodium products are not used, unless otherwise indicated.

- Solid vegetable shortening (not butter, margarine, nonstick cooking sprays or vegetable oil spread as they can cause sticking problems) is used to grease pans, unless otherwise indicated.

Equipment Used in Recipe Testing:

We use equipment for testing that the majority of consumers use in their homes. If a specific piece of equipment (such as a wire whisk) is necessary for recipe success, it will be listed in the recipe.

- Cookware and bakeware *without* nonstick coatings are used, unless otherwise indicated.

- No dark colored, black or insulated bakeware is used.

- When a baking *pan* is specified in a recipe, a *metal* pan was used; a baking *dish* or pie *plate* means oven-proof glass was used.

- An electric hand mixer is used for mixing *only when mixer speeds are specified* in the recipe directions. When a mixer speed is not given, a spoon or fork was used.

Metric Conversion Guide

Volume

U.S. Units	Canadian Metric	Australian Metric
1/4 teaspoon	1 mL	1 ml
1/2 teaspoon	2 mL	2 ml
1 teaspoon	5 mL	5 ml
1 tablespoon	15 mL	20 ml
1/4 cup	50 mL	60 ml
1/3 cup	75 mL	80 ml
1/2 cup	125 mL	125 ml
2/3 cup	150 mL	170 ml
3/4 cup	175 mL	190 ml
1 cup	250 mL	250 ml
1 quart	1 liter	1 liter
1 1/2 quarts	1.5 liters	1.5 liters
2 quarts	2 liters	2 liters
2 1/2 quarts	2.5 liters	2.5 liters
3 quarts	3 liters	3 liters
4 quarts	4 liters	4 liters

Measurements

Inches	Centimeters
1	2.5
2	5.0
3	7.5
4	10.0
5	12.5
6	15.0
7	17.5
8	20.5
9	23.0
10	25.5
11	28.0
12	30.5
13	33.0
14	35.5
15	38.0

Weight

U.S. Units	Canadian Metric	Australian Metric
1 ounce	30 grams	30 grams
2 ounces	55 grams	60 grams
3 ounces	85 grams	90 grams
4 ounces (1/4 pound)	115 grams	125 grams
8 ounces (1/2 pound)	225 grams	225 grams
16 ounces (1 pound)	455 grams	500 grams
1 pound	455 grams	1/2 kilogram

Temperatures

Fahrenheit	Celsius
32°	0°
212°	100°
250°	120°
275°	140°
300°	150°
325°	160°
350°	180°
375°	190°
400°	200°
425°	220°
450°	230°
475°	240°
500°	260°

Note: The recipes in this cookbook have not been developed or tested using metric measures. When converting recipes to metric, some variations in quality may be noted.

Index

Numbers in *italics* refer to photographs.